THE FOREIGN POLICY
RESEARCH INSTITUTE SERIES

The Foreign Policy Research Institute
University of Pennsylvania

NUMBER 1

Perón's fall and the new regime

PRAEGER : NEW YORK

ARGENTINE UPHEAVAL

Arthur P. Whitaker

This volume is the first of a series of studies to be published by Frederick A. Praeger, Publishers, under the auspices of the Foreign Policy Research Institute at the University of Pennsylvania, established under a grant of the Richardson Foundation, Greensboro, North Carolina. This study was subjected to the extensive and critical discussion of the Associates of the Foreign Policy Research Institute. However, the views expressed in ARGENTINE UPHEAVAL: *Perón's Fall and the New Regime* are the author's own.

Contents

PART III
International relations

EPILOGUE

APPENDICES

Introduction

Widely variant interpretations have been placed upon the five months' Argentine crisis from June to November 1955, which led, first, to the overthrow of Juan Perón's ten-year tyranny and its replacement by General Eduardo Lonardi's caretaker military government, and then to the ousting of Lonardi in favor of another general, Pedro Eugenio Aramburu. On one point, however, there seems to be general agreement, namely that this Argentine upheaval has important international implications. These will be stressed in the following pages.

Moreover, even in its domestic aspects the overthrow of Perón possesses great interest for students of totalitarianism as a world problem. This is suggested by the thesis advanced by the leader of the revolution against Perón, General Eduardo Lonardi. Speaking on September 23, 1955, a few days after Perón's fall, Lonardi said:

> "Argentina [on this occasion] gave the world the first example of an absolutely totalitarian government—armed with all the weapons of propaganda and force, and seconded by a misled but important sector of the people—overturned not by a foreign war, but by the people's love for liberty, their heartbeat of honor, and complete sacrifice."

For reasons which will be developed below, Argentina has been a country of rapidly increasing importance to the

United States in recent decades, and a never-failing source
of knotty problems. The recent Argentine upheaval is therefore of special interest to students of the foreign relations of
the United States.

It is from this point of view that the following account
of the upheaval has been written; but as the foreign and
domestic affairs of Argentina are inextricably intertwined,
the following pages will deal at considerable length with
the domestic aspects of the crisis. Also, for reasons stated in
detail elsewhere,[1] the present writer believes that the roots
of both the Perón regime and the major opposition to it in
Argentina lie deep in the Argentine past. Pertinent features
of the background will therefore be indicated below, though
only the briefest indication will be possible within the limits
of the present study.

This broad approach seems all the more necessary as an
aid to understanding the Argentine situation because of the
unexpected suddenness of Perón's overthrow, which came far
earlier than most observers had predicted. One of these was
the present writer, who, in a book published in December
1954, wrote: "His [Perón's] hold on the two principal power
groups in Argentina, the armed forces and labor, is so strong
that, barring his resignation or assassination, he may be expected to complete his term [as president] and, in the next
election (1957), obtain the presidency either for himself
or for one of his lieutenants."[2] To be sure, this forecast was
prefaced by the cautionary statement that "Whether that
[i.e., the end of Perón's dominion over Argentina] will come
soon or late, and what will follow it, are questions that only
a seer could answer." It is also true that the forecast was
qualified by the saving phrase "barring his resignation" and

[1] Arthur P. Whitaker, *The United States and Argentina* (Cambridge: Har-
vard University Press, 1954), pp. 24, 30–31, 47, 66, 209–212.
[2] Whitaker, *The United States and Argentina*, p. 246.

that Perón did in fact resign, though he later denied having done so. Nevertheless, the writer is frank to admit that he did not expect Perón's resignation to take place either so soon or under compulsion, as it did.

Another mistaken forecaster was Herbert L. Matthews, of the *New York Times*. On April 6, 1955, at the end of what he described as "nearly two months of intensive study in Argentina," Mr. Matthews gave it as his considered opinion that: "It is first necessary to recognize that the [Perón] regime cannot fall and probably cannot be overthrown . . . With the complete decomposition of the opposition accomplished, no element is in a position to act against General Perón." [3]

Accordingly, in the hope of rendering more intelligible with the aid of hindsight a course of events that was so little expected, the following study of Argentina's latest revolution will begin with a review of the three-months crisis from the abortive naval revolt against Perón on June 16 to his overthrow on September 19. A similar review will then be given of subsequent events in Argentina under the caretaker government headed successively by Generals Lonardi and Aramburu, down to December 1, 1955, which is the terminal date of the present study. These narrative sections, which are continuous, form the first of the three parts into which the following study is divided. Part II analyzes the major classes, power groups, and political parties in present-day Argentina, and Part III deals with the foreign policy of the new Argentine government as it had developed by our terminal date, and its international implications, particularly from the point of view of the United States.

It is almost superfluous to say that this study makes no pretense to definitiveness, or even to complete accuracy,

[3] This article, the first of four on the situation in Argentina, was dated Santiago, Chile, April 6, and published in the *New York Times* for April 10, 1955.

though every effort has been made to present the facts as accurately as possible. As regards the Perón period, the main obstacle lies in his government's suppression of free speech and restrictions on foreign correspondence, which made it difficult to know just what was going on in Argentina and still more difficult to know just what the Argentine people thought about it. The lifting of the lid after Perón's overthrow freed the flow of news from Argentina, but at times restrictions have been reimposed and at the present writing the reports are still confused, contradictory, or silent on some important points. Confronted with this situation, the foreign commentator is liable to give credence to those reports which are in harmony with his prepossessions. As these vary considerably from one commentator to another, the diversity of interpretations of the current Argentine crisis is hardly surprising. The writer does not flatter himself that the present study is an exception to the rule, though he has done his best to make it one.

The materials on which this study is based include communications from anti-Peronista sources in Argentina while Perón was still in power, conversations with persons, both Argentine and non-Argentine, who have been in that country since June, 1955, and the U.S. Department of State's reports of monitored radio broadcasts from Argentina and neighboring countries, as well as newspaper reports and magazine articles.

PART I

*From tyranny to caretaker
government*

1. The background of the revolt of June 16

The Argentine revolt of June 16, 1955, lasted less than half a day, but it appears to have been the most serious threat Perón had faced since he emerged as the strong man of Argentina at the end of the critical nine days from October 9 to 17, 1945. On the latter occasion Perón, then only a colonel and *primus inter pares* in a two-year-old military dictatorship, made a hairbreadth escape from political disaster and won control of Argentina by forcing upon his reluctant fellow Army officers an alliance with the *descamisados* or "shirtless ones," the masses of Argentina organized in captive labor unions. From that time forth this Army-labor alliance remained the principal support of his power.

Elected President of Argentina in February 1946 and re-elected five years later, Perón established and maintained a nationalistic, demagogic, authoritarian regime. He labeled his system "justicialism" and gave it the motto "Political sovereignty, economic independence, social justice." This ostensibly meant that the Argentine people were to be freed from domination and exploitation by the "imperialist" nations (Britain and the United States) in league with Argentina's own former ruling class, the "oligarchy." To give the devil his due, Perón's vaunted "social revolution" did confer some benefits on the descamisados, but politically his regime was thoroughly pernicious from the start, and it grew worse every year. It was a quasi-totalitarian tyranny which made a mockery of the democratic ideals it pretended to serve. It suppressed all freedoms, beginning with freedom of speech, hamstrung the opposition parties, and developed a new oligarchy of its own—all under the astute and ruthless personal leadership of Juan Perón. As commander-in-chief of the nation's armed forces [1] and self-styled "the foremost laborer in Argentina," Perón was the personal symbol of the Army-labor alliance on which his regime rested.

From the start, the oppressive and demagogic character of the regime provoked strong opposition in various sectors of Argentine society. Prior to June 1955 this found its most serious expression in a revolt in September 1951 by a part of the Army, many of whose officers had never been reconciled to the alliance of the armed forces with the descamisados. The rebels never had a chance. Poor timing and teamwork among their leaders is said to have cost them the support of other elements among the armed forces as well as among the civilian population, and the revolt was suppressed quickly and almost bloodlessly. Its net result was to tighten Perón's control of the Army, which was purged by the imprisonment of many of its officers, though none of them was put to death. As for the enlisted men, they seem to have been, so to speak, "Peronized" by osmosis, since most of them came from the descamisado masses who were the darlings of the Perón regime.

The circumstances of the June 1955 revolt were quite different, for at first the rebels had complete control of the air and they struck only a few hours after the public announce-

[1] In Argentina as in the United States, the nation's President is also commander-in-chief of its armed forces. This is one of many features of the U.S. Constitution which the framers of the Argentine Constitution of 1853 borrowed and which are still a part of the former as amended under Perón in 1949.

ment that Perón had been excommunicated for expelling two Roman Catholic prelates from Argentina. Although the publication of this ban had not been permitted in Argentina, it had been made widely known there by radio broadcasts from stations in other countries, including Uruguay, just across the River Plate. The effect was electrifying. Under the Argentine Constitution the Catholic Church had been state-supported for more than a hundred years, the overwhelming majority of Argentines are Roman Catholics, and the excommunication came as the climax of a seven-months controversy of mounting intensity between Perón's government and the Catholic Church.[2]

In the early years of his first administration Perón had sought Church support and had met with considerable success in the effort, but a rift began to appear between the two at least as early as 1950. This widened gradually in the next four years, and then, with a suddenness which surprised all known observers, developed into a bitter and violent controversy from November 1954 to mid-June 1955. At first the Church leaders' displeasure was concentrated on certain Peronista measures which, though long under discussion, were now at last enacted, such as the legalization of divorce and prostitution and the secularization (or rather the resecularization [3]) of education. On his part, Perón complained that the Church was playing politics and specifically that it was renewing its alliance with the secular oligarchy or privileged class, which had been one of his main targets ever since the beginning in 1943 of his social revolution in favor of the descamisados. In fact, Perón is said to have been

---

[2] See Appendix 2, Document 1, "Perón on the Church-State Controversy."

[3] Religious instruction in Argentine public schools was prohibited by an Act of Congress in 1883 which soon led to a breach with the Vatican that lasted until 1900. In 1943, under the military dictatorship, the act was rescinded and religious instruction made obligatory; after Perón came to power this decree was ratified by an Act of Congress.

most disturbed over the political activities of certain clerics in quite a different direction—the formation of a Christian Democratic party along popular and quasi-socialistic lines which might enable it to make inroads on his own desca- misado following.

In the early months of 1955 other issues fanned the flames, the battle front widened, and large numbers of Catholic priests and lay leaders were arrested by Perón's police. On May 1 (traditionally one of the great *fiestas* of the descamis- ados) his followers made the conflict total by formally initiat- ing a movement to separate Church and State through a constitutional amendment. The following weeks were marked by ever more violent demonstrations, counter-dem- onstrations, clashes between the rival demonstrators, and an attack on the archiepiscopal palace in Buenos Aires (the aged Archbishop, quite ill, was not in the palace at the time). The breaking point came when the Church authorities failed to obey a government order forbidding a Corpus Christi procession and a riot ensued. Perón retaliated with the ex- pulsion of the two Catholic prelates from Argentina on June 14; they went straight to the Vatican; and on June 16 Perón's excommunication was announced. A few hours later the revolt began.

There is no evidence whatever that the Catholic hierarchy supported the revolt. On the other hand, it appears that naval officers had been planning to rebel for two or three years past, quite independently of the church-state contro- versy. According to one report, what finally brought them to the point of rebellion was a decree requiring all naval of- ficers to take a course of instruction in Peronista doctrine. Nevertheless, there can be little question that the conspira- tors sought to take advantage of the situation created by that controversy. Indeed, it appears that the scale and vio- lence of the anti-Peronista demonstrations which it provoked may have betrayed the conspirators into a feeling of over-confidence which in turn led them to launch the attack prematurely. At any rate, one of their sympathizers stated a few days after the fiasco that the revolt had been planned to take place six days later, on June 22, but that hot-heads among the naval officers and their civilian supporters had jumped the gun. This is easy to believe, for the event revealed the same lack of coordination that had led to the failure of the Army revolt of 1951; and this time the Army in Buenos Aires, where all the important fighting took place, supported Perón.

2. The revolt of June 16 and its sequel

The revolt began at 12:45 p.m. with an attack by Navy planes on the Casa Rosada, or presidential office building, and nearby government strong points such as the headquarters of the General Confederation of Labor, or C.G.T.[4] Almost at once a contingent of marines began a supporting ground action against the same objectives. With some support from the Air Force, other Navy planes attacked loyal air bases, both civil and military, in the neighborhood of Buenos Aires, and apparently immobilized the Army's pursuit planes. Civilian rebels attacked communications centers and for a short time held one of the main broadcasting stations, Radio Mitre, from which they proclaimed a "democratic revolution."

Thanks to the loyalty of the Army, all the ground positions were back under government control in a matter of hours, and while the rebels dominated the air over Buenos Aires all afternoon, their planes had nowhere to land, refuel, and rearm. The descamisados, too, rallied to Perón's defense, but they had few arms and their role was mainly sacrificial. In mid-afternoon, prematurely confident of victory, they swarmed into the wide Plaza de Mayo, on which the Casa Rosada fronts, and were caught there by another rebel air at-

4 See below, pp. 68–71.

tack. Many of the loyalist casualties [5] of the revolt occurred at this time and most of the rest when a descamisado mob attacked the rebel headquarters in the Navy Ministry and was repulsed by machine gun fire. Resentment over these losses may have contributed to the mob attacks which seriously damaged many Catholic churches in Buenos Aires that same night and which also did Perón serious damage by the shock they caused even among lukewarm Catholics.

By 6 p.m. the Army's tanks and armored cars had reduced the rebels' headquarters in the Navy Ministry. The rebel air force, having nowhere else to go, was already beginning to take refuge in neighboring Uruguay. By the next day 39 planes with 122 persons were reported as having arrived. The refugees were ready with explanations of their failure—a fog, they said, had prevented effective bombing of their objectives and the landing of vital reinforcements, and certain Army elements had failed to keep their promise to join in the revolt.

At midnight President Perón delivered a triumphant radio address in which he announced that the revolt had been crushed and the government was in complete control of the whole country. At the same time he proclaimed a state of siege, and during the next ten days he turned over to the Army, under the command of General Franklin Lucero, the task of rounding up rebels and restoring normal conditions in the country. At first this task was carried forward rapidly and apparently with complete success. By June 22 the Army had been sent back to its barracks, and on June 29 General Lucero's special mission was terminated.

The restoration of order, however, soon proved to be only temporary and relative. The reasons were partly psycho-

[5] These are reported to have totalled some 360 killed and 1000 wounded, of which the armed forces account for only 25 and 80, respectively; the rest were civilian.

logical. Encouraged by the sensational character of the revolt, despite the fact that it had failed, Perón's enemies redoubled the rumor campaign, which became a source of grave and well founded anxiety to his government. It was said first that Perón had been supplanted by General Lucero or by an Army junta; then that Perón was going to appoint a new cabinet consisting entirely of Army officers; then, when cabinet changes were in fact made but all the retiring civilian members were replaced by civilians, that each of these would have an Army "adviser" who would make all the important decisions. Rumors that the Navy was still in revolt flourished mightily when a large part of the naval forces put out to sea, and only subsided slightly when the Navy Ministry explained that these were routine maneuvers, planned long since and carried out as a sign that normal conditions had been restored.

Quite aside from rumor-mongering, there were plenty of reasons for the continued state of tension. Chief among these were the forced resignations of two top-flight Peronista leaders: Angel Borlenghi, Minister of Interior and Justice and reportedly the Number Two man in the regime, and Eduardo Vuletich, Secretary General of the C.G.T. Since both had been closely identified with the anticlerical campaign that had brought the Church-State controversy to a head, their ejection could be interpreted as meaning nothing more than that Perón had decided after all to make peace with the Church. On the other hand, since both men also represented the descamisado, civilian wing of the regime, their going could be, and in some quarters was, interpreted as signifying a revolutionary alteration of the whole character of the regime, which had hitherto been a joint descamisado-Army affair but would henceforth, it was alleged, be controlled wholly by the Army. This view gained some support from Perón's speeches in the week following the revolt, in which, while praising the descamisados for their loyalty, he gave the Army virtually all the credit for smashing the revolt.

Finally, there came the strange silence of Perón himself. That he should ever be silent was strange, for in the past he had always delivered at least one highly publicized radio address every day; but after stating in a broadcast on June 23 that only his "great will power and sense of duty" had kept him from resigning after the revolt, he had not another word to say for nearly two weeks, while rumors of great changes impending flew thick and fast. Then, on July 4, the state radio announced repeatedly that he would break his silence at noon the following day. Naturally, the rumor campaign snowballed, and, as the *New York Times* report from Buenos Aires stated, "Tension in this city mounted today to its highest pitch since the revolt of June 16." The most widely credited rumor was that the speech would announce Perón's resignation. The rebels, it seemed, though they had lost the battle, were winning the campaign.

This turned out to be wishful thinking. When Perón gave his eagerly awaited speech the following day (July 5), it contained not a word or even a hint of his resignation. It was, however, an exceptionally conciliatory speech. He absolved the opposition parties of the charge, which he had levelled against some of them just after the revolt, of complicity in it, and then went on to ask them for "a truce in the political fight." With a repetition of the familiar slogan, "From home to work and from work to home, and eternal vigilance," which was addressed primarily to his descamisado following, Perón concluded his speech.

Its tone was confident, but the fact that it was conciliatory was taken by his foes as a sign of weakness. Consequently, instead of grasping his proffered hand of friendship, they bent every effort towards undermining his position. The

Radical Party led off the same evening by replying through the Directive Board of its National Committee that "there can be no pacification without liberty" and by asking that its chairman, Arturo Frondizi, be given time on the state radio network to answer Perón's speech.

When the request was at last granted, Frondizi minced no words in his speech (July 28).[6] "Pacification," he said, "cannot and must not be a new form of submission . . . [and] can come about only by fulfilling a group of objective conditions that will restore morality and democracy to the country." He went on to specify certain "concrete measures" which were "indispensable." These added up to a formidable indictment of the Perón regime. They included the restoration of the full effectiveness of the Constitution, beginning with an immediate and ample political amnesty and the lifting of the "internal state of war" (a kind of martial law, in effect since 1951); the eradication of "the mass of corruption which envelopes the life of the country" and its replacement by "republican austerity"; the "return of the freedoms" of speech, press, assembly, association, and religion; the restoration of "full autonomy" to the labor unions and the universities, of justice in the courts, and of "the federative and communal bases of our political system"; the repeal of the current election law and the adoption of "new systems of polling"; an end to the use of schools for Peronista propaganda and to the persecution of teachers, students, artists, and intellectuals; and "the defense of economic sovereignty," beginning with the "rejection of the proposed agreement with a foreign [i.e., United States] petroleum company, because this agreement . . . accepts the regime of foreign strategic bases and crosses the southern part of the national territory with a wide colonial zone."

[6] See Appendix 2, Document 2, "Frondizi's Reply to Perón's Pacification Offer."

This last point, which was aimed against a pending contract of the Perón government with a subsidiary of the Standard Oil Company of California, was pressed vigorously and successfully by Frondizi and other oppositionists in the next two months. It appears to have been one of their most lethal weapons in this last stage of their war on the Perón regime.

However admirable Frondizi's program might have been, it hardly provided a sound basis for cooperation between the Perón regime and the Radical Party. It was, of course, not intended to do so. The Radicals were resolved upon a fight to the finish, although by this time Perón had made (July 15) still another conciliatory move by proclaiming the end of the revolution which he had begun a decade earlier and the restoration of the full effectiveness of the Constitution, which he admitted having taken liberties with when it was necessary to do so in order to carry out his revolution. As an earnest of his sincerity, he resigned as head of the Peronista Party, saying that he wished henceforth to be the leader of the whole nation rather than only a part of it, though that part comprised the overwhelming majority of the Argentine people. The Radicals, however, had no faith in his sincerity and they were justified by the event. What Perón's promise of pacification was worth was shown on the day following Frondizi's speech: the speaker was haled into court on the old familiar charge of *desacato* (disrespect) of Perón.

A more formal reply to Frondizi was given on August 3 by the new head of the Peronista Party, Alejandro H. Leloir. As a lawyer and landowner, Leloir came of a class (the oligarchy and its professional fringe) most of whose members were opposed to Perón. Perhaps for this reason, or perhaps merely because the still ostensibly irenic Perón told him to do so, Leloir gave as soft a reply as Frondizi's blast permitted. He confessed that "our [Peronista] movement is not invulnerable to criticism," that it had made "many mistakes," and that it had at times taken "extreme measures," though only in self-defense; and he also said that "from the standpoint of doctrine, the position taken by the [Radicals] coincides with that of our movement," and that the difference between Radicals and Peronistas was mainly one between words and deeds. But his patience soon wore thin and he charged Frondizi with falsifying history in support of his allegations of Peronista fraud and corruption. "Does he not know," asked Leloir, "that we govern by the will of the immense majority . . . ?" His speech still extended the olive branch, but less unreservedly than before, and while it was still extended with an air of self-confidence, the gesture was still regarded by the opposition as a sign of weakness of which quick advantage should be taken.

Only three additional illustrations of the opposition's attitude will be given here. First, on August 6 four national associations of Argentine doctors, dentists, engineers, and lawyers joined with Buenos Aires Bar Association in demanding the repeal of a law of 1946 which placed them under government control, thereby, they complained, curtailing "the constitutional right of free association" and contravening "the fundamental principle of self-government." The engineers also issued a separate statement which went even further, charging that their association, "once the pride of Argentina and its members," had been wrecked by official control and that "individual engineers have been submitted to pressure, tortured, or thrown into jail."

Then, on August 10, Dr. Vicente Solano Lima, speaking for the National Democratic (Conservative) Party let loose a blast against the Perón regime that fell little if any short of the Radical Party's in explosive power. But he added a new note in his denunciation of the government's anti-clerical campaign. "A destructive principle is menacing Argentine society, as is shown by the unusual conflict provoked with Catholicism," he declared. ". . . The religious conflict hides the political purpose—one more step ahead by the State to do away with resistance to its all-engulfing empire . . . Stripped of his attributes as a human being, [man] is defenseless and is exposed to the materialistic tendencies of extreme leftist ideologies which threaten to revive ancient slavery."

The third illustration is provided by the series of night attacks on individual members of the police force which began in mid-July and continued at the rate of four or five a week through August. Individually, they were made on too small a scale to be anything but a nuisance to the government, but they were so uniform and systematic that they were obviously designed to undermine it by intensifying the atmosphere of insecurity and alarm.

In short, the course of events during the six weeks following Perón's conciliatory speech on June 5 made it increasingly clear that his call for a "political truce" and "coexistence" was not going to be accepted by the opposition on terms to which he could consent. That being so, it would be suicidal for him to continue in the state of dependence on the Army alone to which he had been reduced since June 16.

3. The descamisados again

Accordingly, from mid-August to mid-September Perón sought to shore up his regime by reviving the features that had characterized it before June 16 and which the revolt of that date seemed for several weeks to have altered profoundly if not destroyed—its tough, repressive attitude towards the opposition; its maintenance of an equal balance between its two main power groups, the Army and the descamisados; and its anticlericalism, which, though not an original feature of the regime, had clearly begun to take shape several years before the controversy that led to Perón's excommunication in June 1955. Yet no two situations are ever quite the same, as Perón was to learn to his cost in mid-September.

On August 15 the police announced that they had discovered and foiled a plot to assassinate Perón, and hundreds of arrests were made. Simultaneously, one of Perón's own former associates, ex-Under Secretary of Foreign Affairs Mario Amadeo, created a sensation by addressing a public letter to the Under Secretary of the War Department urging the Army, which had saved Perón on July 16, to save Argentina from Perón by overthrowing his regime and restoring constitutional government.

In the face of this situation the governing council of the Peronista Party announced on August 17 that it regarded the political truce as ended and that it had decided to "renew in full force the brilliant political movement of 1946 in which the people, disgusted by fraud, oppression, and misery, determined to have a government of their own and to that end elected Perón." Asking whether the anti-Peronistas really believed, as they were suggesting, that "President Perón's head would be given them as the price of peace," the statement continued: "We have already made it clear that we will not yield an inch of ground to those who, forgetting that they are Argentines, are trying to destroy the constituted authorities and to exploit confessional questions for exclusively political purposes." The implication of this reference to "confessional questions" was made clear the same day by the Peronista newspaper *Democracia*, which asserted that the assassination plot just revealed "is much graver than the revolt of June 16 because it was hidden behind clerical cassocks." This sort of thing, the writer warned, "could require repressive measures such as the Argentine people have never needed until now."

The views of the government (now nominally divorced from the Peronista Party) were stated the following day, August 18, by Oscar Albrieu, Minister of the Interior in succession to the notorious anticlerical and descamisado spokesman, Angel Borlenghi. Albrieu's emphasis was different from that of the Peronista Party council, but his warning was equally firm. To him, the villain of the piece was not the Church but the old oligarchy, for he asserted that "what the current anti-government demonstrations are directed against is the social conquests of the people effected under the Perón government." He continued: "The time has come for the government to warn that tolerance has reached its limits and that the government's mission is to maintain order . . .

Two or three hundred families [*i.e.*, the oligarchy] cannot be permitted to keep in a state of turmoil nineteen million Argentines whose desire is to live in peace and security."

The events of the next ten days pointed in different directions, thereby deepening the confusion. On the one hand, the number of political casualties among the leadership of the regime was brought to six by the "resignation" of Jerónimo Remorino, who as Minister of Foreign Affairs and Public Worship, had been responsible in some measure for the anticlerical campaign that preceded the revolt of June 16. His successor, Dr. Ildefonso Cavagna Martínez, was a conservative untainted by anticlericalism. The change seemed to indicate that the regime would continue to follow its new policy of moderation, in this respect at least. On the other hand, it seemed to be preparing for more trouble. To the older Federal Security Council, presided over by the Minister of the Interior (a civilian), there had recently been added a National Security Board (*Junta Nacional de Seguridad*) and this was now placed under the command of an Army officer, fifty-year-old General Félix Robles, former military attaché of the Argentine Embassy in Washington. This Board was given control over the Federal Police, the National *Gendarmería,* and the Maritime Prefecture—that is, all the forces of public order in the country except the Army, Navy, and Air Force, which had already been purged and reorganized by Perón just after June 16.

Meanwhile, the night attacks on the police continued. On the night of August 26 one was made on two guards at the residence of U. S. Ambassador Albert F. Nufer, who was commonly regarded as a friend of Perón's. Likewise, verbal attacks on the regime continued. On August 26, fifty-six former labor leaders (who had been ousted by Perón) issued a statement in which they charged that the labor movement in Argentina had lost its independence since

1943—a fact well known but seldom publicly stated in that country—and that labor's "lack of autonomy" was "one of the fundamental factors in the present national crisis."

The boldness of the ex-labor leaders' statement made it a threat to the regime at one of its most vital points: its control over the phalanx of captive labor unions in which the descamisados were organized. If that control were lost, Perón would have no other important power group on his side except the Army, which, though it had saved him on June 16, might get out of hand unless it were counter-balanced, as formerly, by the descamisados. The Army had sought to turn him out in October 1945 and would have succeeded but for the marshalling of the descamisado hosts on his side on the famous October 17. Part of the Army had risen against him once more in September 1951 and had again been checkmated by his descamisado support. A year later the descamisados in turn had to be curbed lest they become too strong, but now the roles were once more reversed, for since the revolt of June 16, 1955, the balance of power between the two had inclined heavily in favor of the Army. The balance must be restored at all costs, for it was the very foundation of the Perón regime.

This situation probably explains the next scene in the drama, and the most spectacular of all that had taken place since the revolt of June 16. This scene, another descamisado show of strength, took place on Wednesday, August 31, from early morning to midnight. Perón and the other actors in it played their parts with carefully prepared spontaneity and obviously followed a script inspired by the events of the famous October 17, 1945, when the descamisado hosts rescued Perón from the oblivion to which he had been consigned by the Army.

The play opened at nine o'clock on the morning of August 31 with a radio broadcast in which Héctor Hugo di

Pietro, secretary general of the General Confederation of Labor, read a letter from President Perón offering to resign the presidency.[7] Repeating the assertion he had made in July that his revolutionary program had been carried out, Perón's letter continued:

> "The time has passed for reforms and strife. Now work and consolidation must be achieved . . . I believe the moment has come to offer my resignation if it would be a guarantee of pacification . . . To achieve definitive pacification, other men whose strength has not been spent in the effort can advantageously replace me ₄ . . We, as profound reformers, find difficulty in being good pacifiers and stabilizers . . .
>
> "Some thoughtless and speculative politicians . . . speak of civil war. There will be no civil war here. There will be peace or dictatorship.
>
> "I do not have the character to be a dictator, so that if such an eventuality should occur, another or others will have to replace me . . . I humbly ask the millions of Argentines who have trusted me to free me from all commitments and accept my departure from the Government, so that I can take my place as a simple Peronista in our Movement."

This letter was addressed to the two branches of the Peronista Party (men's and women's) as well as to the C.G.T., for, concluded Perón, "it is from them that I derive the corresponding authority to act in the manner of which I have spoken."

All three organizations of course rejected the offer and immediately set in motion the machinery for a mass protest by the descamisados that same night.[8] A general strike order

---

[7] See Appendix 2, Document 3, "Perón's First Resignation Offer."
[8] See Appendix 2, Document 4, "C.G.T. Rejects Perón's Offer," and Document 5, "Peronista Party Calls for 'Another October 17.'"

by the C.G.T. released the workers for it, and by special trains, buses, and trucks the faithful were brought to the city from the interior as well as from the metropolitan area of Buenos Aires.

As on the fateful October 17 ten years earlier, though reportedly in smaller numbers, they all converged on the Plaza de Mayo, crying "We want Perón!" Again Perón addressed them from the familiar balcony of the Casa Rosada, whose still obvious battle scars of June 16 now provided another and much more recent memory to excite the indignant loyalty of his followers. And again, as on that October day, Perón played the part of the reluctant leader yielding to popular clamor for his guiding hand. In short, he now withdrew the offer to resign which he had made only twelve hours earlier.

There were, however, important differences between both the circumstances and the tone of the addresses on the two occasions. In 1945, though he had just snatched victory from defeat after having been forced to resign, his speech breathed a confidence so complete that at the end of it he bade his followers to take time off for a celebration and rest, as he himself planned to do. In 1955, on the other hand, he only made an offer to resign, which was withdrawn after it had aroused a ritual protest, and his speech to the faithful in the Plaza de Mayo was not a paean of victory but a call to battle. In fact, this speech is the most incendiary he has ever made. Admonishing the descamisados to "annihilate and crush" any one who tried to deprive them of the social gains they had obtained under his leadership, he specified:

> "From now on let us establish as permanent conduct for our Movement that he who in any place tries to disturb order in opposition to constituted authorities or contrary to the law or the constitution may be slain by any Argentine . . . And when one of our people falls, five of them will fall."

Such words would have come naturally at any time from Perón's late wife, Eva, glamorous but vitriolic and ranting Jacobin and high priestess of the descamisado cult, but on the lips of Perón himself they were strange and shocking. After his victory in the crisis of October 1945 he had left it to Evita to tear passions to tatters while he himself spoke in a manner befitting his lifelong career—that of an officer and a gentleman. After her death in 1952 he had no trouble in finding worthy successors to her in rabble-rousers of the type of Borlenghi and Vuletich, so that in his own speeches he was left free to go on playing his serener role, as he did past the middle of 1955. Even at the height of the Church-State controversy in May and early June, and again on the morrow of the revolt of June 16, his speeches breathed the spirit of moderation, order, peace, and coexistence. Obviously, he was now deliberately shifting to the oratorical style of his late wife. But why? Was it because he felt sure of his position once more—so sure that he could afford the luxury of venting the spleen against his adversaries which he had had to pen up since June 16? Or was his speech a desperate bid for descamisado support, made because he now realized that even the Army was turning against him?

Still a third explanation, which seems the most plausible of all, may be given: Perón was neither over-confident nor desperate, but he was psychologically the captive of his victory in October 1945, which he now tried to repeat, not only in the same place and manner, but with essentially the same end in view. That end was the two-fold effect that a demonstration of his descamisado strength would have on the Army, first by insuring the Army's loyalty to him and second by setting up a counterpoise to the Army in his regime.

The rationale was the same on both occasions: a descamisado demonstration would warn the Army that if it tried to overthrow Perón, the result would be civil war and a national bloodbath. In 1945 this device had worked to perfection. Perón evidently thought it would work again. That was the worst mistake he ever made and it was fatal. Disaffected elements in the Army, which were now numerous, saw as clearly as Perón did that another October 17 would probably mean another ten years of Perón, and rather than submit to that they were willing—as they had not been in 1945—to risk a national bloodbath if there was no other way of destroying the Perón regime.

Though fatal, his error was natural and perhaps unavoidable. If it was induced by the psychogical compulsion of the October 17 pattern, it also rested on rational grounds. Perón evidently thought that at this particular moment it was more important for him to conciliate the descamisados than the Army, for he could not have failed to realize that his highly inflammatory speech of August 31 would offend many Army officers, most of whom came of respectable middle class families. Consequently, in making the speech he was taking a coolly calculated risk.

Perón's next step, taken the following day (September 1), was to have his compliant Congress reimpose a state of siege in Buenos Aires,[9] where most of the turmoil since June 16 had taken place and where the only important opposition party, the Radicals, had their stronghold. Under the state of siege, all civil rights were suspended, the military were authorized to search and seize arms without a court order, the establishment of censorship was authorized, and the President was empowered to arrest any person and banish him to any designated point in the interior of the country. Thus ended the brief experiment with pacification, mutual understanding, and coexistence inaugurated by Perón in his speech of July 5. The votes on the passage of the bill

[9] The state of siege imposed on June 16 and lifted on July 5 had applied to the whole country.

showed that his control over his followers in both houses of Congress was unshaken: In the Chamber of Deputies the bill passed by 109 votes (all Peronista) to 12 (all Radical), and the solidly Peronista Senate thereupon approved it unanimously.

President Perón officially promulgated the law early on September 3, and General Robles, as National Director of Security, promptly published a list of offenses under it, which, he warned, would be punished "with maximum severity and energy." The list gives some idea of the nature of the controls thus established. It included interference with production, commerce, and transportation; the spreading of rumors; the printing, dissemination or possession of subversive or tendentious publications; the importation or possession of unauthorized weapons; unauthorized meetings; and "offenses" as well as attacks against the armed forces or the police.

This was quickly followed by two other important steps. Later the same day, a house cleaning was started in the Peronista Party, of which Perón himself had been frankly critical when he resigned the leadership of it in July. Speaking in the city of Eva Perón (formerly La Plata) on September 3, the new head of the party, Alejandro Leloir, announced the beginning of an "inexorable purge" of the party to rid it of its "weaklings and traitors."

Four days later came one of the most significant steps of all. On September 7, the governing council of the General Confederation of Labor announced that it was "offering" its 6,000,000 members to the Army as a civil militia, "so that, when necessary, they can be utilized in defense of the law, the constitution, and constituted authorities." What the announcement tactfully called an offer might better be described as an admonition to the Army to remember that the C.G.T. contained 6,000,000 potential fighters on Perón's side.

The issue was not a new one. In 1952, towards the end of Eva Perón's life and with her aid and that of her henchmen, the C.G.T. actually started building itself up into a para-military organization with armored cars and anti-tank guns. Just after her death that was stopped by Perón, who was then swinging from the political left to center, and who in any case was as unwilling to have the balance upset in favor of the descamisados as of the Army. More recently, the Army had taken advantage of the opportunity offered it by the revolt of June 16 to seize the C.G.T.'s comparatively small remaining arsenal of some 5,000 rifles and revolvers. Now, however, Perón urgently needed to fortify his des-camisado phalanx, and the C.G.T.'s "offer" of September 7 may therefore be regarded as the second step (his speech of August 31 was the first) in the resurgence of the descamis-ado factor in his regime.

The resurgence was so quick, and by this time so nearly complete, that one is entitled to have some doubts about the accuracy of the reporting from Buenos Aires earlier in the year about the state of relations between Perón and or-ganized labor. Before June 16, this ran to the effect that he was losing the support of labor; after June 16, that he had either lost it or, under intimidation by the Army, was afraid to mobilize such of it as still remained to him. For a time, his silence gave some plausibility to the latter report, but this was shattered by his demagogic speech of August 31. In reporting the C.G.T.'s "offer" of its 6,000,000 militiamen a week later an Associated Press despatch from Buenos Aires stated without qualification that: "The C.G.T. is the back-bone of President Juan D. Perón's strength . . . Observers consider that it at least rivals, if it does not surpass, the Army as a power factor in the nation."

It soon proved, however, that the resurgence of the des-camisados and, through them, of Perón's own power was more apparent than real, and that he had fatally under-estimated the strength with which the Army would react against it. Even the faction in the Army most loyal to him turned thumbs down on the C.G.T. militia proposal; its rejection was announced on September 8 by none other than General Franklin Lucero, Perón's own Minister of War and leader of the Army elements that had intervened decisively in his favor on and after June 16.

Meanwhile, disaffection among the armed forces, which had long been rife in the Navy and Air Force, spread rapidly in the Army, above all in its numerous elements that were stationed outside the Federal District of Buenos Aires. To be sure, all this while an increasingly vigorous effort was being made under the direction of General Lucero himself to detect and stamp out disaffection in the Army. Thus, on September 14 a Radical deputy formally requested a congressional investigation of the arrest in the last four days alone of 40 high-ranking Army officers, and Reuters, in transmitting this news item from Buenos Aires, commented that it "gives weight to widespread reports of Army unrest." General Lucero, however, seems to have repeated the error that was made when the revived state of siege was confined to the Federal District of Buenos Aires. As a result, disaffection flourished in the provinces, whose weight proved to be decisive.

The first evidence of serious Army disaffection in the provinces came on September 8 with the announcement of the frustration of a conspiracy centered in the Río Cuarto Army base in the interior Province of Córdoba. According to a detailed account of the plot published in the *New York Times* on September 13, there was to have been a "large-scale military rebellion in Córdoba Province," headed by General Felix Videla Balaguer and involving three regiments in the capital city of the same name and one at the Río

Cuarto base one hundred miles away, but the plot was revealed by an unidentified major and broken up by timely police action. On the other hand, an ambush laid for the ringleaders was frustrated when they in turn were warned in time to make their escape. In Córdoba Province, it seemed, neither side could keep a secret.

The chief beneficiaries of this sieve-like security situation were the anti-government forces, for the escaped ringleaders, headed by General Balaguer, were able to maintain contact with their fellow-conspirators in other parts of Argentina. Events moved quickly, as they had to if the provincial conspirators were to escape being picked off piecemeal by Perón and Lucero from the nation's central strong-point, Buenos Aires.

4. Perón's fall

The final revolt began on September 16, three months to a day after the abortive revolt by parts of the Navy and Air Force. This time, too, it was essentially the work of the armed forces. Civilians had little part in it, except in the Catholic city of Córdoba, and the numerous police forces seem to have remained loyal for the most part. But this time it was supported from the start by most of the Navy—not merely by its Air Force, as on June 16, but by the warships as well—by most of the Air Force, and by a considerable part of the Army; and other important Army elements joined in it when it was not promptly suppressed.

Historically, the most striking thing about this revolt is not that it overthrew the ten-year-old regime of Perón but that it ended the seventy-year-old domination of the rest of the country, "the interior," by Buenos Aires. Down to and including the federalization of the city of Buenos Aires in 1880, many of the most important decisions in Argentine public life had been thrust upon the city by "the interior," but since that date the rule had been that "as Buenos Aires goes, so goes the nation." The revolution of September 1955 restored the earlier pattern, even to the extent that the tyrant Perón was overthrown, as his political ancestor the tyrant

Rosas had been in 1852, by the interior, though both still had firm control of Buenos Aires.

The decisive role played by the interior in ousting Perón was the result of deliberate planning by the rebels. As General Lonardi explained in his first speech in Buenos Aires (September 23) after victory: "The concentration of [Perón's] forces in the Federal capital made it very difficult to deal the initial blow there. It was therefore necessary to deal it in the interior and with the aid of the Navy. Córdoba, Cuyo, and the shoreline provinces were [accordingly] selected as the primary bases . . ."

One of the two main revolutionary centers was Córdoba, which is Argentina's third largest city and lies some 300 miles northwest of Buenos Aires in the northern "interior," the oldest settled part of Argentina. The other, which lies some 400 miles south of Buenos Aires, was the two-headed center formed by the naval base at Río Santiago and the nearby seaport of Bahía Blanca, whose 100,000 population makes it one of the nation's chief provincial cities. These two centers had the disadvantage of being widely separated. On the other hand, the combined attributes of the two made them representative of almost every aspect of the nation's life. Traditionalist Córdoba was the focus both of Argentine Catholicism and also of a rich agricultural-pastoral community, though it had recently made some beginnings in industry (one of the most recent was a Henry J. Kaiser plant). On the other hand, commercial and maritime Bahía Blanca was a product of the modern age and above all of the grain trade begun under British stimulus in the late nineteenth century.

In this sense the revolt was truly national from the beginning, but it was far from being nationwide. Not only was it, as already mentioned, the work of a part of the armed forces, with little active civilian participation, except in

Córdoba, but up to the moment of Perón's resignation the forces loyal to him still controlled the country's second largest city, Rosario, and most of the provinces, in addition to metropolitan Buenos Aires, which contains one fourth of Argentina's 19,000,000 inhabitants.

Yet, whereas the revolt of June 16 was suppressed in a matter of hours, the revolt begun on September 16 overthrew Perón in four days. Subject to correction when the facts are more fully revealed, we suggest that the three crucial events were the failure of the government forces sent against Bahía Blanca and the Río Santiago naval base to press the attack vigorously; the successful holding action of both civilian and military rebels in the Córdoba area in the face of the very strong attack made on them by loyalist troops; and the threat that rebel warships would bombard the city of Buenos Aires.

The Bahía Blanca-Río Santiago operation remains at the present writing the most obscure of these three events. It is still difficult to say whether the weakness of the government forces' action here was due to lack of zeal or outright sympathy with the rebels or logistic difficulties, or to a combination of the three. Whatever the reason, the government's failure to respond vigorously to this challenge gave a heavy blow to its prestige and encouraged the defection of waverers to the other side.

In sharp contrast to the government's ineffectual action against Bahía Blanca was the rebels' heroic and successful fight against great odds in Córdoba. Doubtless because the revolt had been proclaimed from Córdoba and this city was the largest in rebel hands, the government concentrated its major efforts here, and it was able to act quickly because it had been alerted in this zone by the recently exposed military plot. At first the loyalist forces carried everything before them and within twenty-four hours they announced

that the revolt in Córdoba had been crushed. The announcement was premature, for two resistance forces in the area
still held out. One was in the city itself and consisted mainly
of civilian volunteers, led by a few regular soldiers, who
kept up a house-to-house fight. The other, at an Army base
a few miles outside the city, consisted mainly of cadets and
was led by General Eduardo Lonardi, an anti-Peronista
career soldier who had been forced into retirement after the
Army revolt of 1951, had conspired tirelessly since then, and
had proclaimed the present revolt at Córdoba on September
16.[10] This little band not only fought off all efforts to reduce
it but also used its handful of military planes to carry the
war to the enemy and give encouragement to the resistance
forces in the city.

The effect was much wider than that; in fact, the success
of these two Córdoba groups in holding out against the
far superior government forces seems to have played a large
part in bringing about on September 18 an important Army
defection to the rebel side. The defectors included all the
Army units in the San Juan-Mendoza area of western
Argentina along the Chilean frontier. This almost completely
cut off loyalist Argentina from the outside world, for on the
east it was already bottled up by a naval blockade, and a
large part of the Air Force was on the rebel side. Moreover,
this defection brought within sight an alignment of the
armed forces in all the rest of the nation against those in
the Buenos Aires area.

Civil wars of this type had been fought in the nineteenth
century, but now there was a new factor—a navy able to
inflict enormous damage on the exposed 'city of Buenos
Aires, and by its own declaration quite willing to sacrifice
the nation's capital as the price of victory over Perón. As
an earnest of its intentions, the rebel naval command, headed

[10] See Appendix 2, Document 6, "Lonardi Proclaims 'Liberating Revolution.'"

by Admiral Isaac Rojas, did bombard the seashore resort city of Mar del Plata as the fleet moved from the South Atlantic into the broad estuary called the Río de la Plata (River Plate), on which Buenos Aires fronts.

For a night and a day Perón and his generals ignored rebel threats that the same treatment would be administered to Buenos Aires and to the capital of the province of that name, the city of La Plata, which had been renamed Eva Perón. But as the augmented fleet moved into position in front of him and the defection of the Western Army signalized the crumbling of his forces in the interior, Perón on September 19 again offered to resign. The offer was made in an open letter "To the Army and the people of the nation" which was read over the Argentine state radio by General Lucero. In it Perón expressed confidence in the ability of the Army and the people to put down the rebellion but said that he wished to spare the nation a civil war and the city of Buenos Aires a bombardment, and accordingly suggested that the Army "take charge of the situation" and "seek pacification . . . before it is too late."

This time his proffered resignation was accepted forthwith and the government was taken over by a Military Junta consisting of four generals, all loyalists, of whom Lucero was not one. The Junta lost no time in seeking a pacification, which it obtained at the end of three days of confused negotiation by turning over the government to the rebels. Perón himself had already taken refuge on a Paraguayan gunboat at Buenos Aires under the right of political asylum. After a fortnight's delay, he was permitted to fly to Paraguay itself,[11] from which on November 1 he left by air for Nicaragua.

That the strong forces holding the nation's capital sur-

11 For a discussion of this episode and the right of asylum, see below, pp. 116–118.

rendered so tamely is easier to understand in the light of the magnanimous and conciliatory spirit shown by the rebels in victory. "In this revolution," they said, "there have been neither victors nor vanquished." A striking example of this spirit was given by the chief of the revolution, General Lonardi, at Córdoba. There a loyalist force had defended its position with great courage and tenacity, and when it surrendered, Lonardi had his own victorious troops "pass in review before the defeated troops as a gesture of tribute and admiration" and then let the losers remain under parole in their own barracks, where he ordered them to be "treated with the respect and consideration that these valiant soldiers of the fatherland have earned." Here was an analogy to Grant's treatment of Lee's defeated Confederates at Appomattox.

5. The caretaker government: Lonardi

It remained to be seen whether General Lonardi's desire for magnanimous reconciliation would prevail more successfully in Argentina than General Grant's did in the United States in the Reconstruction years just after Appomattox. The hope that it would do so found support—perhaps its chief support—in the character and views of Lonardi himself and in a lesson of history, for Lonardi was high-minded, courageous, and sincerely desirous of internal peace, and the irenic policy which he counseled had been followed with considerable success after the overthrow of Argentina's first tyrant, Rosas, in 1852.

The new regime was headed by General Lonardi, with the title of Provisional President, and Admiral Isaac Rojas as Vice President, but both apparently had to act within the broad limits set by a military Junta consisting of fourteen high-ranking Army, Navy, and Air Force officers. Accordingly, the caretaker government was—unavoidably, it would seem—a military dictatorship. Nevertheless, Lonardi began by giving most of the posts in his cabinet to civilians, by restoring freedom of speech and the press, and by promising to restore fully constitutional government through free elections to be held as soon as possible. He even fixed an approximate target date for these elections: some six or seven months ("180 to 220 days") from the beginning of his administration, or in other words, about April or May 1956.

Late in October Lonardi gave added weight to the civilian element in his regime by establishing a National Consultative Council consisting of twenty members who represented all the political parties except the Communists and Peronistas. Those represented in it were the Radical, National Democratic (Conservative), Progressive Democratic, Socialist, and Christian Democratic parties and the Christian Democratic Federal Union. Leaders of all the parties represented in the Consultative Council had already rallied to the support of the Provisional Government. Conspicuous among them was the noted Socialist leader Américo Ghioldi, who in a radio speech on October 13 said:

> "This revolution is not one of a party, a church, an army, a faction . . . It is a liberating revolution which separated the diseased head of the tyranny from the sane body of the nation . . . Because this is a liberating and not a dogmatic revolution, all problems which tend to divide democratic people must be set aside."

These were brave words, but no liberating revolution was ever without its dogmas, and in Argentina these brought about another overturn within a month after Ghioldi spoke.

Lonardi's views on the problems immediately confronting him augured well for the success of his policy of conciliation. They were stated in a speech broadcast on September 23 from Buenos Aires, to which he had just transferred his government from its first seat in Córdoba. After some introductory remarks about the recent revolution, he described "the program of my provisional action." This, he said, "can be summed up in four words: the rule of right." Particularizing, he outlined the following policies:

(1) In the economic field he promised "to end inflation through a reduction of the bureaucracy," which under Perón had become "a parasitic and useless agency." Existing "pacts" would be honored, but the pending petroleum pact with a subsidiary of Standard Oil of California would be re-examined since "according to authoritative sources . . . [it] is not advantageous to us."

(2) "The rights of the Church and everyone's religious conscience, regardless of their creed," would be guaranteed and "all differences" with the Catholic Church would be settled "through the conclusion of a concordat." Education, "on which the future of our nation hinges," would be purged of the propaganda infused into it by Perón and the universities would be made as autonomous as possible.

(3) "The rights of assembly, association, and of the press will be restored immediately . . . Nobody will be molested for criticizing me . . . Nowhere in the world will [the press] enjoy more genuine freedom."

(4) ". . . The labor unions will be free and the legitimate gains of the workers will be maintained and expanded. Along with that of my comrades-in-arms, I desire the cooperation of the workers . . . They will always have in me a father or brother."

(5) He concluded by appealing to his "comrades-in-arms" to make "the greatest possible effort and sacrifice in order to restore the prestige of the armed forces" and to "carry out with modesty and decorum the assignment of protecting the laws."

This was a high-minded as well as a conciliatory program and parts of it were promptly carried out. Thus, the "rights of assembly, association, and of the press" were in fact restored immediately, and if the autonomy of the universities was not also re-established at once, they were at least placed under the interim administration of the right kind of "inter-ventors," such as the distinguished and courageous anti-

Peronista intellectual, José Luis Romero, who was given that post in the University of Buenos Aires.

Nevertheless, it soon became clear that Lonardi did not possess the magician's wand which alone could still the turbulence that has tossed the Argentine nation ever since 1930 and which shows no signs of abating. Before a fortnight had passed, it was a matter of public knowledge that opposition had developed against him even within the armed forces, which were the only direct support of his dictatorship. As early as October 2 an Associated Press despatch reported that "Army resentment over the influence of the Navy in the new Government was high" and that "some Army men" were planning "a palace coup" against Lonardi. Added to this were the surviving strength of Peronismo, the continuing controversy over Church-State relations, and other stresses and strains among the parties and classes of Argentina, of which we shall speak more fully in Part II.

An immediate problem of the greatest gravity was posed for the new regime by its heritage of economic ruin from Perón. If ruin seems too strong a word, it does not suggest a darker picture than the one painted by General Lonardi himself in a radio broadcast to the nation on October 26.[12] Using data assembled by his special economic adviser, Raúl Prebisch,[13] he devoted his entire speech to what he described as "the gravest problem before us, namely, the economic situation." "Ten years of irresponsibility and corruption," he continued, "have carried us to a most disastrous situation in the economic field . . . If anyone had undertaken the task of purposely wrecking our economy and annihilating its dynamic forces, he could not have accomplished it in a more complete manner." Most of the rest

[12] See Appendix 2, Document 7, "Lonardi on the Disastrous Economic Situation."
[13] See below, pp. 109–110.

of the speech documented these charges in detail. Solutions were discussed more briefly and in rather general terms, and the nation was warned not to expect miracles, but rather to brace itself for a regime of austerity.

The solemn tone of Lonardi's address was only too well justified. He might be suspected of exaggerating economic difficulties for political effect, but they were undoubtedly serious and they were sure to aggravate the political and social problems which he already faced. It was the masses, among whom Peronismo was strongest and loyalty to the new regime weakest, who were likely to suffer most in the period of austerity that Lonardi forecast for the nation.

Moreover, by November 1 Lonardi had shown some signs of changing the character of his provisional, caretaker regime and he had definitely hedged at some points on his policy of conciliation.

In considering whether the character of Lonardi's Provisional Government changed in this period, one must keep three aspects of it in mind: the extent of the powers that it assumed, its use of these powers, and its views regarding its own duration. As to the first of these, no change was perceptible. Indeed, there was hardly any room for change except in the direction of abandonment, for from the start he assumed not only executive but legislative power; promptly dissolving the Peronista Congress, he legislated by decrees having the force of law. He also reconstituted the Supreme Court by executive fiat, dismissing four of the five Peronista judges and filling their places with his own appointees. By contrast, when Perón purged the Supreme Court in 1946 to make way for his own appointees, he used the slower process of impeachment, as provided by the Argentine Constitution; but Lonardi had no Congress to assist him, and everyone seems to have agreed to forget about the Constitution at this point.

The question of the Provisional Government's use of its powers must be broken down into two parts. The first has reference to Lonardi's initial policy of reconciliation, of "neither victors nor vanquished." In his first full press conference on September 28, he made this more specific by saying that under his regime "no discrimination will be made against Peronistas" and that he had no intention of "intervening" the General Confederation of Labor (G.G.T.), which we have seen was a Peronista stronghold. Subsequently, however, Peronista labor leaders were arrested, Peronista Army officers were retired, and the two Peronista political parties were dissolved. The climax came when on October 28 officials of all unions composing the C.G.T. were suspended by the government and new elections ordered, and when on October 29 an investigating commission set up by Lonardi declared guilty of treason not only Perón himself but all the Peronista members of Congress (numbering more than 300) who had voted for laws subverting the Argentine Constitution, and recommended that they be imprisoned for life. All this may have been quite necessary and proper, but it did not breathe the regime's original spirit of national conciliation and no reprisals.

The second part of the question is whether Lonardi's government used its powers in a way appropriate to its provisional, "caretaker" character, or whether it went beyond this into a field that ought to be reserved for a constitutional, democratically elected government. The line may be a difficult one to draw with any degree of precision, but Argentines who supported Lonardi whole-heartedly—such as the leaders of the big Radical Party—insisted that it could be drawn and must be observed. To a foreign observer, it would seem that Lonardi did more than might be expected of a caretaker government. Three illustrations, all of which will be discussed below in Part III, are its decision to ratify the Bogotá Charter of the Organization of American States, its project for a concordat with the Vatican, and its venture into the field of comprehensive, long-range economic planning. Measures of this type seemed to indicate a disposition in the Provisional Government not merely to take care of the house, but to remodel it.

The third part of this question relates to the life expectancy of the Provisional Government. The answer here is that General Lonardi did not decree an extension of its life beyond the period originally set, but became less precise about the date of its termination. At the outset, on September 24, he fixed this date within narrow limits by stating that the national elections which were to choose a constitutional government to replace his Provisional Government would be held within a period of "from 180 to 220 days" from his taking power. On October 19, however, he replied to a question on this subject that he could not say when the elections would be held and could only point out that it would take quite a while to draw up new lists of voters and complete the other necessary preparations. On the other hand, about the same time he gave explicit assurance that no member of his government would be a candidate in these elections.

We may conclude, then, in the light of Lonardi's brief record, that the present Provisional Government, like the military dictatorships of 1930 and 1943, will probably last longer and do more than it promised at the outset, but that it will not try to perpetuate itself in power, as both of them did. Rather, we have been given no reason to doubt that, in what it considers due time, it will do its best to re-establish constitutional, democratic government in Argentina. The best warranty for this is the promise given by President Lonardi and renewed even more emphatically by his successor in the provisional presidency, General Aramburu. The next best warranty is that many Argentines in various social sectors seem to have learned a salutary lesson from their country's unhappy experiences of the past quarter century with assorted forms of class rule and authoritarianism.

6. Test cases: C.G.T. and La Prensa

It was already clear by the end of October that Lonardi's task was going to be a very difficult one. Some of the reasons were peculiar to Argentina and some even to this moment in its history, such as the turbulence that had become traditional in that country since 1930, the continuing strength of Peronismo after Perón's fall, and the apprehensions felt even by non-Peronistas that the new regime would not keep Lonardi's promise to preserve the social gains made by the masses under Perón. Most of the underlying causes of the difficulty, however, are not peculiar to that country, but are shared with many other countries in various parts of the world. Indeed, insofar as these causes are economic and social, Argentina, as a country of "intermediate" development, has a double share of them, combining as it does the causes of unrest in developed countries such as France and Italy with those in underdeveloped countries such as Iran, India, and Guatemala.

As the best way of showing the difficulty of Lonardi's problems and of indicating his approach to them, let us examine two test cases. One involves the six-million-strong General Confederation of Labor (C.G.T.), long a tower of Peronista strength; the other, the once great liberal newspaper, *La Prensa,* whose anti-Peronismo led in 1951 to its expropriation by the government, which then sold it to the C.G.T.

Since the crucially important problem of the C.G.T. will be discussed in some detail in Part II, we shall here only summarize the main stages of the case as it had developed by November 1. In the first stage the Provisional Government promised to keep hands off organized labor and did not dare to touch even the Peronista leaders of the C.G.T. The very same Hugo di Pietro who had set the stage for the descamisado demonstration and Perón's incendiary speech on August 31 was permitted to continue as its head, and in that capacity to negotiate with President Lonardi as if he had been the ambassador of a foreign power. In the second stage, the government, now surer of itself, encouraged the piecemeal ousting of Peronista leaders by anti-Peronista members. This process reached its climax on October 25 with a government order suspending all officers of the C.G.T. and calling for new elections. The third stage opened on October 31. Obviously reacting against the government's attrition tactics, the C.G.T. high command on that date ordered a nation-wide general strike on Wednesday, November 2, in support of its demand for an ouster of the anti-Peronista leaders installed in many unions during the second stage. How Lonardi's indecisive response to this challenge hastened his fall will be related below.[14]

One of the concessions made by Lonardi in his negotiation with Hugo di Pietro had been the promise to leave the C.G.T. in undisturbed possession of the newspaper *La Prensa,* pending the adjudication of the case by the courts. This concession came as a severe shock to liberals both at home and abroad, because of the high standards of journalistic competence and integrity which the old *La Prensa* had

[14] See below, pp. 47–48.

maintained for many years before its seizure by Perón, because of what its seizure symbolized, and because under C.G.T. management it had been converted into one of the chief journalistic props of Perón's tyranny. Consequently, it had been widely expected that Lonardi would restore *La Prensa* to its former owners forthwith. The disillusionment caused by his decision not to do so was little mitigated when he pointed out (quite correctly) that the legal questions involved were very complex and explained that he had no choice but to leave the case of *La Prensa* for settlement by the courts of law.[15] Observers noted sourly that means were being found at this time to return to their former owners other confiscated or expropriated newspapers which the powerful C.G.T. had not acquired.

Whether Lonardi's decision in the case of *La Prensa* was right or wrong, it has a significance far greater than that possessed by any Argentine newspaper or all the country's newspapers combined, for it touches upon almost every aspect of the life of the whole nation. Its significance lies in the fact that what had been suffered by *La Prensa*—injustice under a veneer of legality—had also been suffered by millions of Argentines in every walk of life, from businessmen, professional men, school teachers, and landowners, to members of the very class that Perón professed to serve most devotedly, the workingmen and women. If the wrongs done to these millions of people over a period of ten years were to be righted by the process prescribed by Lonardi in

[15] There is a difference of opinion as to whether Perón's seizure of *La Prensa* should be called "expropriation" or "confiscation." The *New York Times* for September 27, 1955, commits itself to both of these opposing views, its news despatch from Buenos Aires by Sam Pope Brewer stating flatly that the Peronista authorities "expropriated it [La Prensa]," and its editorial of the same date, "La Prensa—The Symbol," stating categorically that *La Prensa* "was in fact confiscated, not expropriated." The present writer prefers "expropriation," but, not being a lawyer, would leave the question to those versed in the law, specifically Argentine law.

the case of *La Prensa,* then a tremendous strain would be imposed on the courts of Argentina and on the patience of the millions involved. For many, moreover, judicial remedy could not begin until Peronista laws had been changed; there was no Congress to change them since one of Lonardi's first steps had been to dissolve the Peronista Congress; and at least six or eight months must elapse before a new one could be elected, after which there would be a further delay before the new Congress could be installed and begin its long task of cleaning the Augean stables.

What was the alternative? Was the Provisional President to supplant both the Congress and the courts, and, after legislating by decree, then administer executive justice? In that case he would be continuing and perhaps exceeding Perón's own violations of the Constitution and the laws. Moreover, his "courts" would become as crowded as the regular courts of law on our first hypothesis. Or was he to prevent overcrowding by closing his doors to the little sufferers until he had given redress to the big sufferers such as the ousted owners of *La Prensa?* In the long run that could hardly prove a sound beginning for the democratic regime which it was Lonardi's professed purpose to re-establish.

Given Lonardi's legalistic approach to the problem, there was in fact no satisfactory solution, and it remained for his successor, General Aramburu, to cut the Gordian knot by decreeing the restoration of *La Prensa* to its former owners.[16] That may have been the best solution, but it

16 Nevertheless, Aramburu too had qualms about the Constitution and the laws and on November 23 he announced that "the National Consultative Council [see above, p. 35] is now entrusted with the study of the legal status of the Government." Its study will add a new chapter to the history of that interesting Argentine phenomenon, the constitutional law of revolution, to which important chapters were contributed by the revolutions of 1930 and 1943.

should be remembered that, important though it was, the case of *La Prensa* was only a small part of the complex and enormously difficult problem of righting the wrongs of a decade of Peronismo. The problem is one which seems likely to vex the Argentine people for a long time to come.

7. Changing caretakers: Aramburu

By November 1 the Appomattox spirit of reconciliation was all but dead and on the thirteenth Lonardi, who had embodied it, was forced out of office by his associates in the caretaker government. He had responded in some measure to the growing demand for a sterner policy of "de-Peronization," but his response was not sufficiently quick and decisive to suit his associates. While many issues were involved, such as the prosecution of former Peronista officials and of Army officers who had turned Perón's favors into fortunes, discontent on this score seems to have been brought to a head by Lonardi's handling of the C.G.T. strike on November 2. On the one hand, Lonardi succeeded in getting the C.G.T. leaders to call off the strike and to agree to the holding of elections by the membership under military supervision, and on November 4 the appointment of the first 80 military commissioners for this purpose was announced. On the other hand, Lonardi agreed that in the meanwhile Andrés Framini and Luis Nattalini, both of whom were tainted with Peronismo, should retain their posts as joint general secretaries of the C.G.T.

"It is believed," said one report of this settlement, "that the agreement will lead to stormy debates and protests" since anti-Peronista labor leaders were determined that "Nattalini and Framini must get out." The forecast was quickly borne out by events, all the more so because it was clear that Nattalini and Framini did not control even the Peronistas in the C.G.T., many of whom stayed out on strike even after their leaders had given the "back to work" order. Moreover, the Peronistas seemed to have been emboldened by the settlement, for on November 7 they staged a public demonstration at the San Isidro racetrack, where they greeted President Lonardi and Vice President Rojas with catcalls and showers of stones, invaded the racetrack, and shouted "Perón, Perón!" "Tear gas," says the report, "had to be used to end the tumult." Anti-Peronistas felt that the time had come for a showdown and that Lonardi was not the person to force it.

The other main ground of dissatisfaction with Lonardi was the presence of reactionary elements in his government, as represented by Foreign Minister Amadeo and the head of the Press and Cultural Relations Office, Juan Carlos Goyeneche, who had served Perón on a cultural mission to Franco Spain in 1948. Lonardi's brother-in-law, Clemente Villada Achaval, was also regarded as a member of this group.

Both issues were given a public airing on November 3 in a radio address by one of the most outspoken Radical leaders, Ernesto Enrique Sammartino. Born in 1902, Sammartino had achieved prominence in the law and journalism as well as politics; ever since the early 1930's he had taken a leading part in the fight against Fascist-Nazi-Falangist forces in Argentina; and in 1948 he had been expelled from the Peronista-controlled Chamber of Deputies for an exceptionally violent speech against the regime. From that time until shortly after Perón's overthrow he had lived in exile in Montevideo. Now he was back again, still fighting

Fascism in all its forms with undiminished vigor. In his radio speech on November 3 he said:

> "In the underground of the [present] revolution two counter-revolutionary forces are moving in silence . . . One of these forces is represented by the remains of the overthrown regime, the C.G.T. and many unions . . . together with the political organizations of Peronismo . . . The Government has acted with too much trust toward this counterrevolutionary reaction, and thus has helped the saboteurs at their task . . . The second conspiracy . . . is that nourished by reactionary forces of dogmatic and fascist mentality. This second counterrevolution, that of Argentina's medieval period, is more dangerous than the first. It has its black popes and its brown-shirted strategists . . . They know that they will not reach power by the honest road of votes, but they believe in the miracle of electoral combinations and in the providential help of generals who admired Hitler and who served Hitler's favorite pupil, Perón, until the Navy trained its guns on him . . . The plans of these forces will not have the compliance of the Provisional President or the Vice President . . . but [they] bank on the good faith of the Government and on its difficulties. Above all they have an unexpected ally: disputes within the Radical Party."

The speaker then pled with his fellow Radicals to forget their doctrinal differences with one another and unite for the salvation of freedom in Argentina. "Otherwise," he warned, "we shall have to resign ourselves to live again under the whip of military regimes and the despotism of scholastic dogmas and economic privilege."

Before another week was out, the government crisis began its rapid development. On November 8 came the resignation of the Minister of the Army, General León Bengoa, who had been accused of laxity in "de-Peronizing" the Army. The same day three meetings behind closed doors were held by leaders in the government and the armed forces, and it was rumored that Lonardi was about to resign. The following day Goyeneche resigned, to the great satisfaction of liberals and anti-clericals; but three days later Lonardi reversed his course and virtually forced the resignation of an outstanding liberal member of his cabinet, Eduardo Busso, by reducing him from Minister of Interior and Justice to Minister of Justice alone. This was widely regarded as a victory for the reactionary Catholic group, and all the members of the Consultative Council, except those representing the Christian Democratic Federal Union, resigned in protest.[17]

On the following day, November 13, Lonardi was overthrown by a palace coup. At 4 p.m. General Pedro Eugenio Aramburu announced that Lonardi had resigned and that he himself was now Provisional President. As finally worked out by the end of the day, control of the new regime was vested in a five-man military junta headed by Aramburu and including the three heads of Army, Navy, and Air Force, and Admiral Rojas, who stayed on as Vice President. At 8 p.m. Lonardi issued a statement denying that he had resigned and asserting that he had been ousted by the "decision of a part of the armed forces"; but he made no appeal to arms and so this revolution, Argentina's second in eight weeks, was a bloodless one.

Indeed, according to Aramburu, there had been no revolution at all, but merely a restoration of the "liberating revolution" of September to the path of democracy originally planned for it.[18] Lonardi himself, the official version ran, was a fine man, but he had permitted himself to be surrounded

[17] For the Consultative Council, see above, p. 35.
[18] See Appendix 2, Document 8, "Aramburu Supplants Lonardi," and Document 9, "Why Lonardi Was Ousted." This interpretation was designed in part to prevent the question of recognition by foreign governments from being raised. It was successful in doing so. See below, p. 124.

and misled by "small but very influential groups" which "represented the strongest reaction," were "identified with totalitarian ideologies," and had "tried to take refuge behind the banner of our Catholic institutions." The new regime, Aramburu promised, would "reestablish the reign of law and return the country to genuine democracy" under the leadership of "men who, throughout their lives and on their past record, constitute the most solid guarantee of the fulfillment of their aims."

The members of the Consultative Council, representing most of the country's political parties, promptly withdrew the resignations which they had submitted to Lonardi and gave Aramburu a warm endorsement. On the other hand, the C.G.T. leaders, who knew what was in store for them as well as for the reactionary Catholic groups, as promptly retorted with an order for a general strike on November 15. This was the showdown at last, and the Aramburu government was ready for it. Recognizing the right to strike, but only as a last resort, it declared this strike illegal, arrested Nattalini and Framini and more than a hundred lesser leaders, stationed tanks and armored cars at strategic points, and had detachments of soldiers "rough-up" anyone inciting the workers to strike. It also established censorship of the press, and took drastic action against two newspapers, *La Prensa* and *El Líder*, which were still controlled editorially by the C.G.T., though their business management had recently been taken over by the government under Lonardi.

Even at the start the strike was supported only by the industrial workers, and their enthusiasm for it quickly broke down under the heavy pressure exerted against it by the government. After only one day it was clear that the strike had failed, and Aramburu quickly followed up his advantage by "intervening" the C.G.T., that is, placing it under a government administrator. The person chosen for this post was a naval captain, but he was made directly responsible to Aramburu's new Minister of Labor, Raúl C. Migone, a recognized authority on labor problems and in pre-Perón days a representative of Argentina in the International Labor Organization. There was room for doubt whether Migone was the best man for the job, for Argentine labor leaders were quoted as describing him as "more at home in a library than on a picket line" and he had been out of the country for the past ten years. At any rate he was strongly anti-Peronista—that is why he had been in exile—and so one could be sure that the C.G.T. would no longer serve as an organizational framework for the perpetuation of Peronismo in Argentina.

At the same time the C.G.T.'s loss of *La Prensa* was made definitive and Aramburu declared that he would very soon return it to its owners. This he did by decree on November 30. On December 1 Alberto Gainza Paz, former director of the paper, arrived by air from New York to take charge of it again. On November 30 Aramburu also decreed the abolition of the men's and women's Peronista parties, thus formalizing a decision already announced by Lonardi.

In dealing with the other major threat, that from reactionary forces, Aramburu's procedure was less spectacular and of a piecemeal character. Foreign Minister Amadeo was dismissed and his place filled by Luis A. Podestá Costa, a well known diplomat and authority on international law. Goyeneche, already dismissed just before Lonardi's fall, was arrested. So also, on November 18, were three priests and ten Catholic workers, on the charge of distributing anti-government pamphlets. Two days earlier, in what was described as "one of its rare public statements," the Council of Roman Catholic Bishops in Argentina had stated that the Church had nothing to do with political demonstrations against the government.

More will doubtless be heard about Church-State questions as time goes on. Just before Lonardi's fall, the same council had presented him with a formal request for the abolition of several Peronista measures offensive to the Church, including those legalizing divorce and secularizing education, and it would be surprising if the request were not renewed.

On the labor front, too, important questions remain to be settled. One of the few high officials of the Lonardi regime continued in office by Aramburu was Raúl Prebisch, as economic and financial adviser to the President.[19] In this connection it may be noted that, according to a *New York Times* dispatch sent from Buenos Aires on November 19: "Despite assertions of the Aramburu government to the contrary, labor feels it is in for a hard time under the austerity plan of Dr. Raúl Prebisch . . . Dr. Prebisch is one of the grand targets of [Argentine] labor today and the Communist party is exploiting this fact to the utmost." Moreover, as the exiled Perón has noted with glee, all labor contracts in Argentina expire in February 1956 and the workers will probably demand wage increases to offset the rise in prices which is expected to result from the devaluation of the Argentine peso just after Perón's fall; but the government, which is committed to a national program of austerity, could hardly look with favor on such a demand.

These are only a few of the perplexing problems which face the Aramburu military dictatorship and will face its putative democratic successor at an early date.[20] Under a democratic regime, the chief responsibility for solving them

[19] For Raúl Prebisch, see below, pp. 109–110.
[20] In addition to renewing Lonardi's promise to restore constitutional, democratic government at an early date, Aramburu indicated in a speech on November 23 that he planned to make extensive use of the National Consultative Council, which represents most of the country's political parties. See Appendix 2, Document 10, "Aramburu's Policies."

will fall on the country's political parties. The defects of
these parties were a major factor in opening the way for
Perón a dozen years ago. Are they better able to cope with
the hardly less difficult situation facing their country today? [21]

[21] We may cross our deadline of December 1, 1955, to note two important
statements on the economic crisis by members of the Aramburu government.
In a speech on "Industry Day," December 8, the Minister of Industry said
that there would have to be an increase in prices but that there must be no
increase in wages except in return for increased production. He proposed in
effect a piece-rate system and continued: "Whatever the political evolution
may be, two years are needed to get adequate economic machinery in action
. . . [and] the industrialists and workers will have to bear the main burden
during these two years." On December 15, Economic Adviser Raúl Prebisch
made a public statement to much the same effect, though he stressed the
share of the burden to be borne by the industrialists through a reduction of
their profits. Significantly, he felt it necessary to deny the charge that he
was unconcerned about the welfare of "the laboring masses."

PART II

Classes, power groups, and parties

1. Problems of measurement

The difficulty of measuring the relative strength of political groups is very considerable in any country even under the most favorable circumstances, as when the problem is one of polling opinion about parties in a free and orderly country. The classic illustration of this fact is provided by the presidental campaign of 1948 in the United States, for there is no country in which the appropriate techniques have been more highly developed or more frequently applied, and on that occasion the situation was about as simple as one could imagine, since only two parties of any consequence were involved and these two had been the country's only major parties for generations past. Yet despite these highly favorable circumstances, when the votes were counted, the forecasts of all the leading public opinion polls were shown to have been wrong.

In Argentina such measurements are not only difficult but impossible to make and one must be content with estimates and approximations. The main reason lies in the authoritarian nature of the regimes (not only Perón's, but its predecessors as well) under which Argentina has been governed for the past twenty-five years. This period opened in September 1930 with the overthrow of the 14-year-old Radical government—the most democratic government

Argentina has ever had—by an Army revolt. Thereafter the country was ruled by the following regimes: until early 1932, by a military dictatorship; from 1932 to June 1943, by a conservative civilian minority which kept itself in power by force, fraud, and corruption; from June 1943 to June 1946, by another military dictatorship, of which Juan Perón was a member; and from June 1946 to September 1955, by the nominally constitutional and democratic government headed by Perón as President, which was actually a quasi-totalitarian tyranny.

The present Provisional Government is a military government and it has stated (on reasonable grounds) that the first elections cannot be held before April 1956. In any case, it has been in power so short a time, and the situation in Argentina is still so turbulent and confused at the present writing, that it is almost as difficult now as at any time in the past twenty-five years to measure the relative strength of political groups in that country.

Twenty-five years under such regimes not only made the task of measuring public opinion extremely difficult, but also changed the nature of the thing measured. Lord Acton's dictum that "absolute power corrupts absolutely" is true not only of the ruler but also of the ruled, since force breeds force and oppression breeds conspiracy among the oppressed. Consequently, public opinion in the Argentina of the past quarter century has been something increasingly different from public opinion in freer countries such as the United States and Britain. Probably the most important difference consists in the fact that the element of force which underlies all political activity has become a far more important ingredient of politics in Argentina than in freer countries. We have sought to stress this fact by including "power groups" in the title of the present section. Let it be added at once, however, that we interpret "power" broadly to include spiritual as well as material power, and faith, tradition, morale, and dynamic ideas as well as airplanes, warships, and the big battalions of the Army and organized labor.

It should also be emphasized that, despite the difficulties described above, the task of estimating the strength of power groups and parties in Argentina is by no means a hopeless one and can rise well above the level of guesswork. At no time in this quarter century has power been absolute in Argentina. Even Perón, who made it most nearly absolute, never dared to throw off all controls. To begin with, the Army and labor, which were the two main supports of his power, also set the limits within which he had to exercise it. Moreover, he was the captive of his fiction that his regime was constitutional and democratic. As a result he was hampered by the necessity of doing lip-service to legal and constitutional norms, of holding nominally free elections, and of permitting the opposition to operate openly through organized political parties. To be sure, he used force and fraud to the extent required to insure the continuance of his regime, with the result that every conceivable index of public opinion was distorted in some degree. Yet, since a considerable measure of freedom did exist, the distortion was not complete, so that by correcting the available indices in the light of what we know about the social structure of Argentina and the events of the Perón era, we can arrive at estimates which probably approximate the true situation during the Perón era and the brief period since Perón's fall. This the following pages attempt to do.

2. Oligarchy, middle class, and descamisados

The ethnic composition and class structure of Argentina's present population of some 19,000,000 are largely the product of an economic revolution which took place between 1880 and 1930 under the impact of foreign (mainly British) capital and business enterprise. This was the period when Argentina became one of the world's greatest exporters of foodstuffs (principally beef and wheat) and built the largest railway network in the Western Hemisphere outside the United States (it is still the seventh largest in the world), and when Buenos Aires achieved the rank, which it still holds, of third largest city in the Western Hemisphere, outranked only by New York and Chicago.

This half century of economic expansion attracted to Argentina a flood of immigration—largely Italian and Spanish —which, in proportion to the original population, was even greater than the immigration to the United States at its height from the Civil War to World War I. The change that this brought about in the ethnic composition of the Argentine people was revolutionary. Before 1880, the whites had been in a minority; the majority was made up of Indians, Negroes, and mixed races, among which the *mestizos* (mixed Indian and white) predominated. By 1930, however, Argentina had become whiter than the United States. Ninety percent of its people were now white, only eight per cent *mestizo,* two per cent Indian; and the Negroes had virtually disappeared. Much more important than this change in the color of the skin were the cultural, social, and political changes which it betokened. The traditional "creole" culture was broken down, and the docility with which the creole lower classes had learned to accept upperclass leadership was supplanted by the pretensions of the more dynamic immigrant masses, who insisted that the democratic professions of Argentina's Constitution of 1853 be translated into fact. Thus the stage was set for the turbulent quarter century which began in 1930 and the end of which is not yet in sight.

This turbulence was in part the product of sweeping changes that took place in the same half century from 1880 to 1930 in the class structure of Argentine society. Previously the vast majority of Argentines had belonged to one of two quite simple class divisions: an upper class which had as its core the old "patrician" land-owning families stemming from the colonial period, and a lower class, the gradations within which were important to its members but are not significant for our present purpose. In the boom period after 1880, the upper class, strengthened and enlarged by the enrichment of landowners and stockraisers and the creation of new fortunes in commerce, finance, and industry, became that "oligarchy" so often assailed by Perón; the lower class was profoundly altered by the growth of an urban proletariat and its rural counterpart, who were to constitute Perón's descamisados; and a new class emerged—the middle class, which began to take shape about 1900 and which by the 1940's was reckoned by Argentine sociologists to embrace from 45 to 50 per cent of the country's total population.

Despite its large size, this middle class has failed to

exercise that stabilizing, democratizing influence which most people in the United States seem to expect of any large middle class. The explanation may be found in the fact that in Argentina this class is a mere aggregate of disparate occupational groups and lacks unity, coherence, stability, and morale—that, in fact, it is not a middle class at all, except in the sense that its members occupy a position in between the upper and lower classes. At its lower fringe of small shopkeepers and skilled workers it is scarcely distinguishable from the lower class. At its upper fringe, well-to-do business and professional men aspire to the condition of the oligarchy and look with disfavor on the "pretensions" of labor. Above all, our Argentine sociologists tell us, the members of the Argentine middle class, who are individualists in an age of increasing collectivism, are haunted by a feeling of insecurity. This feeling was intensified among them by the shock of the depression decade after 1929. They had not yet recovered from that when they suffered another shock from the establishment of the quasi-totalitarian, pro-descamisado tyranny of Perón, who professed abhorrence for the "selfish individualism" of the middle class and treated it accordingly.

The character of the Argentine middle class is particularly significant in relation to the officers in the country's armed forces, most of whom have been recruited from that unstable and insecure class. As we have said elsewhere, this fact

> "may help to explain the otherwise puzzling affinity that the officer class of an essentially creole-Spanish-Italian nation have exhibited for the German military training and ideals to which they were systematically exposed for three decades after the first German mission arrived in Argentina in 1911. Perhaps it would not be fanciful to regard affinity for German discipline and authoritarianism as an overcompensation for the insecurity and excessive individualism of

the middle class from which the Argentine officers were sprung and were, so to speak, refugees."[1]

Even if the Argentine middle class had possessed greater cohesion and better morale than it did, it might still have been unequal to the task of keeping the country on an even keel in the quarter century after 1930. Each of the two antipodal classes above and beneath it was strong; each was to prove easier to unite on most of the issues that arose during this period; and their mutual antagonism created a turbulence with which all the disparate middle class elements combined could hardly have coped even if it had not been intensified from abroad by the rising conflict between democracy and Nazi-Fascism. Argentina's important commercial, cultural, and ethnic ties with Europe made her exceptionally sensitive among the Latin American countries to these foreign forces. Moreover, while her own political tradition had been democratic since 1853, this had often been given only lip-service, and its enemies were now encouraged not only by the rise of Nazi-Fascism but also, after 1936, by Franco Spain's propagation of the doctrines of Falangism and Hispanidad, as well as by the even earlier revival of the domestic cult of Argentina's dictator in the generation before 1853, Juan Manuel de Rosas.

In the light of these facts it is not surprising that Argentina has whirled in a political maelstrom ever since 1930. The reasons become clearer if we consider the case of her little neighbor Uruguay, which is just across the River Plate from Argentina, has much the same type of people and economy as Argentina, and since 1880 has been exposed to much the same experiences as Argentina, and which nevertheless has developed politically along lines so widely different from those of Argentina as to be almost

[1] Whitaker, *The United States and Argentina*, p. 14.

diametrically opposite. In the nineteenth century Uruguay, too, had *caudillos* of the Rosas type and these kept the country in a turmoil until 1905, long after Argentina seemed to have settled down under an at least nominally democratic government. After 1880, Uruguay too underwent a rapid economic expansion with the aid of foreign capital and business enterprise and attracted Spanish and Italian immigrants in numbers that were very large in proportion to her original population. Yet politically Uruguay has reversed the Argentine process by developing a regime which has been stable and democratic ever since 1905, with the exception of a brief interlude in the 1930s.

Briefly stated, the reasons for the difference between the two countries seem to be that the area of Uruguay is small and compact, so that its people are more homogeneous than those of Argentina; that the capital of this small country, Montevideo, contains one third of the nation's population and dominates it to an even greater extent than the city of Buenos Aires, with one fifth Argentina's population, does the latter country; and that the people of Montevideo are the chief beneficiaries of a national system of social and labor legislation instituted four decades ago (Uruguay led the Western Hemisphere in this respect), whereas in Argentina little was accomplished in this field until thirty years later under Perón. This fact goes far to explain the latter's hold over the Argentine masses. Had his country followed its little neighbor's example even as late as the 1930s, Perón might never have been heard of outside Army circles; but in contrast to the New Deal in the United States, the Argentine regime during that decade was governed by the "oligarchy," which did nothing to meet the rising demand of the masses for such reforms.

3. Power groups

The class system sketched above is essential to an understanding of the broad sweep of Argentine historical development, especially and increasingly in the twentieth century. In dealing with any given situation, however, one must also take account of the more numerous power groups, some of which cut across class lines in normal times, though in times of crisis they have tended to become identified with one or another of the classes. The interrelationship of classes and power groups will be indicated at appropriate points in the following description of the latter, which applies particularly to the situation as it has developed since Perón began his rise to power in 1943.

THE ARMED FORCES. The Army has a peacetime strength of some 100,000 men backed by several hundred thousand reservists trained under a compulsory system. They are organized in a combat force of a dozen divisions, half of them infantry, the rest partially mechanized. The Navy has a strength of approximately 22,000 men, many of whom are draftees, and some 40 active vessels, which include two battleships, two heavy cruisers, and three light cruisers. The naval air arm has about 100 combat planes with a complement of 1,200 men. The Air Force personnel of about 15,000 mans some 600 planes, a number of which are British-built jet "Meteor" fighters. In addition, Argentina has a national gendarmerie of 10,000 men and 40,000 Federal police.

Before 1930 the armed forces of Argentina were traditionally nonpolitical; that is to say, they regarded politics as the province of civilians and themselves as the servants of the government, not its masters, and accordingly abstained from intervention in the political life of the country. Since 1930, however, that tradition seems to have been forgotten, for the revolutions of that year, of 1943, and of 1955 (the only successful revolts in Argentina since 1852), were all the work of the armed forces. In fact, the latter have abandoned their old tradition in favor of a new one—that of the armed forces as the ultimate arbiter of political disputes in Argentina.

The way in which the armed forces play this role is determined by a number of factors. In the first place, their three main branches are not integrated in any sense, military or political; each branch has its own special character; and in addition to interservice rivalries, there are divisions within each branch, both within the officer group and between the officers and the enlisted men. A few examples must suffice.

The Argentine Army is largely a product of German training, which began about 1900, was intensified after 1911, and continued until 1944. Close ties were also formed with Italy in the 1930s; Perón himself was in that country, as a member of a large military mission, from 1939 to 1941. For reasons that we have already suggested, the middle-class origin of most of the Army officers did not offset these antidemocratic influences. Militarily, the officers have developed a strong *esprit de corps,* but since the Army began to assume a political role, they have been deeply divided in every political crisis save one. They were so divided in the revolutions of September 1930 and September 1955, in the abortive revolts of September 1951 and June 1955, as well as in the crucial week in October 1945 which ended in the triumph of Perón. There is also a division between officers and enlisted men; this was widened under Perón, who was more successful in Peronizing the latter than the former, as evidenced by the abortive revolt of 1951, which was largely the work of some of the officer group and was defeated partly by the loyalty of the enlisted men to Perón. His political shift from left to center after his Jacobin wife Eva's death in 1952 may have weakened his support in this quarter, as it appears to have done among the descamisados at large.

The officers of the Argentine Navy, on the other hand, are reputed to be socially a cut above the Army officers and, beginning in the 1920s, they had as close ties with the United States Navy as did the Army officers with the German Army. In the early months of the military dictatorship set up in 1943 their influence was illustrated by the effort made under the leadership of Admiral Segundo Storni, then Foreign Minister, to align Argentina with the United States and its allies against the Axis; but circumstances forced Storni to couch his overtures in terms unacceptable to the United States, and Secretary of State Cordell Hull rebuffed him so sharply that he was forced to resign, whereupon pro-Axis elements gained complete control of the government at Buenos Aires. From that time until 1955 the Navy played a subordinate role, though Perón gave it token representation in his government by choosing as his second-in-command a retired admiral, Alberto Teisaire, who was 65 years old in 1955. The circumstances of the revolution of September 1955 brought the Navy to the fore again by making sea power decisive, but the new Provisional Government has been headed successively by two Army men, whereas the Navy has had to be content with second place in the person of Admiral and Vice President Isaac Rojas.

What political line the Navy will support is hard to say, for it was clearly divided as recently as the revolt of June 1955 and the rift is not unlikely to reappear. Since the Air Force, too, is politically a doubtful factor and probably not an important one, the Army may be expected to hold its recently regained leadership of the Argentine armed forces in their now traditional role of ultimate arbiter of the country's political disputes.

Despite the fair promises made, and to date largely fulfilled, by the Provisional Government with regard to the reestablishment of constitutional democracy, unbridled optimism is not justified by the precedents set by the Army in the revolutions of 1930 and 1943. On these occasions, too, the Army professed to be the agents of an aroused citizenry in ridding the country of corruption, exploitation, and tyranny and in restoring freedom and constitutional government; and on both occasions what it did was to establish military dictatorships, one of which ultimately gave way to a civilian oligarchy and the other to Perón's regime, of which it was one of the two main supports for ten years. Since history never repeats itself, one can hope, if not for the best, at any rate for something better this time; but the aptitude of the Argentine Army for the decisive role which it now plays in the politics of that country is something that still remains to be demonstrated.

THE C.G.T. (GENERAL CONFEDERATION OF LABOR). The other main support of Perón's regime was the six-million-strong C.G.T. At the present writing this organization has just been "intervened" by the government to purge it of Peronismo, but sooner or later it may be expected to become again one of the major power groups in Argentina.

Founded in 1930, the C.G.T. was small and weak until Perón took it in hand. In 1939 it still had only 263,000 members, mostly skilled laborers; in the next three years it remained static under apathetic leadership; and in 1942 it, along with the other and even smaller Argentine labor unions, was split into two wings, one led by Communists, the other by Socialists. Then Perón took over, expanded the C.G.T. enormously, and made all its members Peronistas. In effect, he used the C.G.T. as a cadre for the mobilization of his descamisados. As an undisciplined mob, the descamisados might have been more of a hindrance than a help to him. By organizing them in the solid phalanx of the captive C.G.T., and giving them for several years material benefits and a sense of their importance such as they had never had before, he built them into a pillar of strength for his regime and at the same time made it far easier for him to manipulate them. This proved to be a masterly device and its success is written over the whole history of his regime.

In this sector, too, as among the enlisted men in the armed forces, Perón seems to have lost ground as a result of his political shift from left to center after 1952, of which he repented too late. There do not, however, appear to have been any mass desertions from his cause before he himself yielded; or if there were, the evidence has not come to the attention of the writer. After his fall, of course, it was another matter, for the support of the C.G.T. and Perón was reciprocal.

His fall raised two interrelated questions about the C.G.T. One was whether the end of the Perón regime meant the end of Peronismo in that organization. The other was whether the Provisional Government would let the C.G.T. manage its own affairs.

A spectacular though appropriately provisional answer was given to both questions by an event that occurred in Buenos Aires on September 25, 1955, and to which we have already referred. That was the occasion on which the Provisional President Lonardi, as one of his first official acts, conferred with the arch-Peronista Secretary General of the C.G.T., Hugo di Pietro, and made several concessions to him. Among these were the controverted promises to let Perón go into exile and to leave the newspaper *La Prensa* in C.G.T. hands pending the adjudication of the case in the courts. Another was the specific application to the C.G.T. of Lonardi's previous general promise not to interfere with organized labor. Evidently the victorious general had a wholesome respect for the continuing strength of the C.G.T. and Peronismo.

Two weeks later matters began to take a different turn when Hugo di Pietro was ousted by his own associates from the post of Secretary General. He appealed to President Lonardi for protection against the allegedly illegal acts of his opponents, but the President refused with evident relish, on the ground that his policy of noninterference with labor worked both ways. But it would be easy to read too much into di Pietro's ouster, for the same *New York Times* despatch that reported it also noted that both members of the duumvirate which succeeded him, Andrés Framini of the Textile Workers Union and Luis Nattalini of the Utilities Workers, were "said to have been identified to some extent with Peronism." Moreover, on the same day pro-Perón leaders of the powerful Meat Workers Union, who had been ejected the day before by anti-Peronistas, regained control of it with the support of a strike by the members and on orders from General Lonardi himself.

We have already related the last acts in this chapter of the C.G.T.'s history—how Lonardi avoided a showdown with it on November 2 and thereby hastened his own fall, and how twelve days later his successor, Aramburu, won a showdown with it and then "intervened" it, thus writing finis to Peronista control of the organization.[2] The workers' response to

2 See above, pp. 51–52.

the general strike order on November 14, which precipitated the showdown, tells a good deal about the surviving strength of Peronismo in the C.G.T. Of its three major groups, two, the commercial and railway workers, ignored the order almost completely, whereas the third, the industrial group (workers in meat packing plants, breweries, tire factories, and metal works) obeyed it almost to a man. This occupational divergence is striking. So also is the overwhelming support given the Peronista leaders of the C.G.T. by the industrial workers in the face of warnings from the military dictatorship and the latter's use of armed force and strong-arm methods in support of its warnings.

Though the picture is still confused, and will probably remain so for some time to come, it would probably be a mistake to write off Peronismo, whether overt or covert, as a force in the organized labor movement in Argentina. It would certainly be a mistake to underrate the strength of that movement. This included only ten per cent of all Argentine workers at the beginning of Perón's regime, but seventy per cent at its end. How the situation will develop depends largely on the attitude of the Provisional Government, and its putative successor, towards labor. Since the present administration is drawn almost entirely from upper and middle-class sources, the outlook for a peaceful development is not very bright. If the Conservatives come to power, as they did after the dictatorship of 1930-31, the outlook will be dim unless Argentina develops a type of "liberal Toryism" which has seldom flourished in that country.

THE OLIGARCHY. We have already spoken of the oligarchy as a class and of the internal divisions from which it suffered. Normally these were serious enough to prevent its component parts from uniting in a single power group. There were exceptions, however, and Perón's social revolution provided one of these, for by forging the unity of the descamisado masses in support of his radical program, he provoked a counter-movement of unification among the upper-class elements that were the main target of his attack. The solidarity of these elements was probably never complete and is not likely to last much longer than the threat that produced it, if only because it never achieved an institutional basis comparable to that which the masses had in the C.G.T. under Perón. In fact, we cannot be sure just how far the unification of the upper class or oligarchy was carried, or how it functioned; this is one of several aspects of the Perón period that are still obscure.

What does seem clear is that the unity and effectiveness of the oligarchy as a power group reached its peak in the last year of Perón's rule, and that it did so because at this time he abandoned the relatively moderate course on which he had embarked after Eva Perón's death in 1952 and renewed the class conflict in terms that made it more threatening than ever before to the traditional institutions and arrangements in Argentina and to their chief beneficiaries, the oligarchy. This was made clear first by his attack on the Catholic Church, beginning in November 1954, and the terms in which he attacked it, and then by his incendiary speech to the descamisados on August 31, 1955. As we have seen, it was this speech, aimed against the oligarchy, that precipitated the final and successful revolt against him, and although it was carried out very largely by the armed forces, we find it hard to believe that members of the oligarchy were not powerful agents behind the scenes. To be sure, there were other agents as well, above all the Radicals; but their agency was notoriously public, it had gone on unbrokenly for a decade, and it had never come anywhere near unhorsing Perón.

THE CATHOLIC CHURCH. Unless the Church-State controversy of Perón's last year in power is viewed in the context which we have just suggested, it is difficult to understand how his attack on the Church could have contributed powerfully to his overthrow, as it apparently did. Alone, the Catholic Church has never carried much weight in the political life of Argentina. Not only has it never been an important power group; there has never been an organized clerical party in that country.[3] To be sure, under a provision of the Constitution of 1853 which is still in effect, the Catholic Church is supported by the Argentine government, but the practice of other faiths is tolerated too, and the situation of the Catholic Church in Argentina is much like that of the Anglican Church in England. Moreover, while the overwhelming majority of Argentines are Catholics, we have it on the authority of Catholic writers that only about 15 per cent of them are active members of the Church. Finally, long before Perón, anticlericalism had flourished in Argentina, as it has done in other Latin countries, and late in the nineteenth century the prohibition of religious instruction in the public schools of Argentina had led to a break between the Vatican and the Buenos Aires government which caused the latter no serious trouble at home though it lasted nearly twenty years.

Yet, one may well ask, if the Catholic Church was not one of the principal power groups in Argentina, why did Perón give his assault on it the highest priority in his whole public program from November 1954 to June 1955? And how could this assault have been a major factor in bringing about his overthrow? Here again we need more information than is now available, but on the basis of such information as we have, it is believed that the following answers are not too far amiss.

To the first question several more or less plausible answers

[3] For the present Christian Democratic parties, which are Catholic but not clerical, see below, pp. 83–85.

have been given. It is likely that more than one of them is correct, for the point at issue is one of motivation and that is usually mixed. One of the most plausible answers is that Perón was countering a recent Catholic move—a move towards the founding of a Christian Democratic Party which might cut into his descamisado following. Another explanation, sponsored by the Radical Party, was that the assault on the Church was simply a diversionary tactic by which Perón hoped to distract attention from unpopular deals by which he was planning to concede oil fields to the Standard Oil Company of California and bases, uranium fields, and sites for atomic experiment to the United States government. Still a third answer, which we have suggested above, is that the assault was a consequence of Perón's swing back to the left; it was certainly popular with the strong left wing of his party. All these answers seem plausible and all are consistent with the view that the Church by itself was not a major power group. An answer which does not seem plausible is that Perón and his associates were offended by the Vatican's failure to take steps towards the canonization of the late Eva Perón—"Saint Eva of America," as her Argentine admirers had dubbed her on their own responsibility. While others may think differently, the present writer cannot see Juan Perón becoming greatly exercised over this issue. Finally, it has been said that this Church-State controversy was simply the inevitable clash of two rival totalitarianisms; but all other objections aside, this explanation leaves unanswered the question why the clash occurred at this time and not one, two, or even five years earlier.

The second question—how, if the Church was comparatively so weak, Perón's assault on it could have been a major factor in his overthrow—is less difficult than it might seem. In the first place, as we have suggested above, part of the answer lies in the terms in which Perón attacked the Church.

What we refer to is the prominence he gave to the charge that the Church, which had cooperated with him in the early years of his regime, had now reverted to its traditional alliance with the oligarchy. By thus bracketing the Church with the oligarchy, he gave warning that his current attack on the former might be only the beginning of his final assault on the latter, which he had hitherto beaten and badgered but had left largely intact. In the face of this threat even the most tepid upper-class Catholics made common cause with the Church, stirred up opposition to Perón in other circles as well, such as the officers of the armed forces, and prepared for a last-ditch stand. In the second place, the Church was the last remaining bulwark of freedom in Argentina, the only institution that had not been brought under Perón's thumb, the only symbol of the old Argentina that had not been prostituted to his service.

Hence it was that the Church issue provided a rallying point for all the enemies of Perón, and this fact alone would have been enough to make the situation the most dangerous he had ever faced, for one of the chief sources of his strength had always been the divisions among his enemies. He had exploited with great success one of the principal political weaknesses of the Argentine friends of freedom, and one which they share with their counterparts in Spain— their inability to unite and work together even against a common enemy. Now at last, however, the most diverse elements rallied to the defense of the Catholic Church. By no means the least of these in strength of numbers and leadership, nor the least surprising as an ally of the Church, was the Radical Party, which throughout the sixty odd years of its life had always been unwaveringly anticlerical.

Thus it was that, thanks to forces stronger than the Church itself, the Church issue aided greatly in bringing Perón's domination of Argentina to an end. The cause of union having disappeared with his departure, the Catholic Church in Argentina may be expected to revert to the subordinate role that it has always played in that country's public affairs. If its role ceases to be subordinate, it is sure to become controversial.

4. Political parties

Following the pattern set by antidemocratic revolutionists in Argentina as well as other countries in the 1920s and '30s, Perón began by trying to destroy the country's whole political party system. His own following, he boasted, was not a party but a national "movement." Though he clung to the use of the term "movement" to the end, his ostensible role as the champion of "true" democracy and the "best" Argentine traditions soon obliged him to abandon the underlying idea in practice and to establish a party of his own. After some experimentation, this finally took shape in two branches, one for men, the Peronista Party (1948), and the other a Peronista Women's Party (1951). The latter was set up under the leadership of Eva Perón, following Perón's extension of the suffrage to women in national elections for the first time in the country's history. Of course both branches of the party were firmly controlled by the government and the two combined won all the elections. In that of 1951, the last general election of the Perón period, they polled an aggregate of about five million in a total of seven and a half million votes cast—roughly a two-thirds majority.

Both Peronista parties survived Perón's overthrow for several weeks, but on October 23 General Lonardi announced that they would be dissolved because they were too "personal" in character to be true political parties and too totalitarian to have any place in a free society. Their dissolution was formally decreed by General Aramburu on November 30.

What, if anything, the now partyless Peronistas will do with their votes in the approaching election is, therefore, one of the biggest question marks in Argentina's uncertain political future. For lack of a better alternative, perhaps many of them will support the Radicals, for despite the bitter antagonism between the two parties in the Perón period, their policies were much alike in some important respects. At the moment, however, any answer to this question must be based mainly on guesswork.

Whatever the right answer may be, the available evidence leaves little room for doubt that Peronismo is still a major political force in Argentina. A week after Perón's flight and at a time when his deserted followers' morale was presumably at ebbtide, the *New York Times* correspondent in Buenos Aires reported that in the opinion of most observers the Peronistas were still the strongest political group in Argentina and would probably win an election if one were held in the near future. Simultaneously, a Radical publication gave similar testimony to the existence of "masses of people who still believe in their runaway apostle" (*las muchedumbres que todavía creen en su apóstol prófugo*).[4] The government itself proved the strength of Peronismo by its acts. On the anniversary of the famous October 17 it adopted severe security measures to hold the Peronistas in hand. It stationed heavily armed troops in the worker districts of the capital, patrolled the streets with ten tanks, served notice on the labor unions that full use of the armed forces would be made to preserve order, and threatened to inflict the death penalty on any demonstrator. That day

4 *Cara o Cruz*, Año 1, No. 9, Buenos Aires, September 1955.

passed without serious disturbance, but a week later it was officially announced that 46 die-hard Peronistas had been jailed in the last 48 hours.

After they have recovered from the shock of their "runaway apostle's" fall and flight, it is quite possible that the Peronistas may become even stronger if the elements now in power adopt the policies one might expect in view of the right-of-center character of the Provisional Government. It is true that at the outset Lonardi adopted a conciliatory attitude towards labor and the masses, but, as we noted in speaking of the C.G.T., even he had begun to get tough with labor before his regime was two months old, and Aramburu got much tougher. In any case, it would take more than words and more even than the weight of a government to allay the social conflict that has been shaping up in Argentina in the past two generations and to moderate the reaction of Perón's victorious enemies against his vaunted social, economic, and political revolution of the past dozen years.

There are of course other Argentine parties besides the two Peronista branches through which mass discontent over such a reaction might express itself. Five of these merit consideration here: the Radicals, two Christian Democratic parties, the Socialists, and the Communists.

The Radical Party (*Unión Cívica Radical* or U.C.R.) is much the strongest of these five and it is virtually certain to play a highly important part in the political life of Argentina in the years just ahead, whatever elements control the government and whatever policies they follow. Ever since its establishment in 1892 the Radical Party has been either the chief opposition party or, as it was from 1916 to 1930, the governing party. Under Perón it was the only opposition party of any consequence and in the last general election, 1951, it polled almost all the votes not cast for him. The number of votes that it gained on that occasion—two and a half million, or about one third of the total—represented a truly remarkable achievement in view of all the handicaps under which the Peronista regime forced it to operate.

How the Radical Party will fare in post-Perón Argentina is another of those questions which the turbulent situation in that country makes it impossible to answer with precision and assurance. Certain major factors, however, are quite clear. On the one hand, the party obviously has important elements of strength. In addition to its historic hold over the loyalties of a large fraction of the Argentine people, it has emerged with great prestige from the long ordeal of the Perón period, during which it was in the forefront in offering courageous and unwavering resistance to tyranny. During that period it also developed a new group of able leaders which is best represented by Arturo Frondizi, chairman of the executive committee of the party's major group and its spokesman in reply to Perón's call for pacification in July 1955.[5] A lawyer by profession and the brother of a well-known philosopher, Risieri Frondizi, who was forced into exile by Perón, Arturo is quiet but forceful, highly intelligent, and an effective speaker whose style suggests the British parliamentarian rather than the Latin orator, and under Perón he had been the embodiment of Radical fortitude in the face of oppression. Finally, the Radicals have the advantage of coming closer than any other party to representing a cross-section of the nation's life, socially as well as geographically. The party has roots in all parts of the country and while its core is middle-class, it has usually had considerable support in the other two classes. Despite its name, it has never until quite recently been really radical but rather a somewhat left-of-center party occupying the middle ground between Socialists and Communists on the one hand and conservatives on the other.

[5] See above, pp. 11–13.

The chief weakness of the Radicals has stemmed from the very fact that the party's membership is broadly representative of the nation, for this has meant that it is also heterogeneous, with the result that tension among its factions has been frequent and schisms not uncommon. A deep and lasting rift opened up in the 1920s between the majority led by Hipólito Irigoyen and a more conservative minority led by the "patrician" Marcelo T. de Alvear. Even in the crisis just before and during Perón's domination the party was again divided over such issues as coalition with other parties and cooperation in Hemisphere defense; and in addition, not a few Radicals went over to Perón. The split has continued to the present writing despite such pleas for unity as Sammartino's,[6] and against the majority or "intransigent" group led by Frondizi is arrayed a more moderate "unionist" group.

The majority Radicals have quite recently adopted two policies which may prove momentous for the party and even for the whole country. In the first place, at the party's national convention on August 12-14, 1955, they took strong measures to enforce discipline and conformity upon the minority group. If this policy is pursued vigorously, it may achieve its purpose of strengthening the party by uniting its factions. On the other hand, it may make the breach permanent and, combined with the second policy, it may bring about the defection of the remaining moderates.

The second policy is the espousal of a program of economic and social revolution, in an obvious effort to win the votes of the now partyless Peronistas. This new policy was given unequivocal expression in the first issue of a periodical launched by the majority Radicals in November 1955 under the title *Causa Obrera* (Labor's Cause). One feature of the issue was a two-column box letter ostensibly written by a Radical workingman, Juan Sincero (Honest John), to his

[6] See above, pp. 48–49.

Peronista *hermano* (brother, fellow workingman), the theme of which was that the Peronista workers, so shamelessly deceived and exploited by Perón, would find their true home in the Radical Party. "Radical workers or Peronista workers, we are all alike," wrote Honest John. "We have the same problems and the same ideals and we ought to struggle together for our rights."

The main feature of this issue, however, was a front-page article on "The Labor Movement and the Social Conquests." The mere preservation of the social conquests made by labor up to the time of Perón's fall, the argument ran, was not enough and must be made only the starting point of a "total and revolutionary change in the bases of the Argentine economy" as an indispensable step towards the achievement of "authentic social justice." The writer particularized: there must be a "vast agrarian reform," including the breaking up and redistribution of estates, and the "principal industries and sources of energy" must be "controlled by the people and directed by organizations which democratically and genuinely represent the people." The enemy, too, was clearly identified: this was the corrupt alliance of foreign "imperialism" and the Argentine "oligarchy," who were hiring conscienceless Argentines of various parties to "defend their antipopular and antinational interests."

To anyone familiar with Perón in his palmy days all this has a familiar sound. In fact, in their effort to catch Peronista votes the majority Radicals seem to be draping themselves in the Peronista mantle, with an appropriate change of labels. Much more is involved, of course, than a mere change of labels, for in honesty and competence the Radical leadership far outshines the Peronista. The result may well be a great Radical accretion of strength. If that takes place, however, and if present Radical promises are kept, there will be more trouble in Argentina. The promised "total and revolutionary transformation" of Argentina's economic and social life will be strongly resisted by many of its people who have no ties with either the oligarchy or foreign imperialism.

While the Radicals' position on foreign policy will be discussed in Part III, it should be pointed out here that this article in *Causa Obrera* indicated a continuation and even a hardening of that antagonism towards the United States which they had manifested for some time past—for example, in opposing the Hemisphere defense system set up by the Rio Defense Treaty of 1947. Obviously, the imperialism denounced in the article was first and foremost Yankee imperialism, and the writer, in boasting of the Radicals' recent resistance to Perón's efforts to "surrender" Argentina's petroleum to "a foreign company," meaning Standard Oil of California, gratuitously described that company as one "of sinister fame." To be sure, Radical leaders profess, no doubt sincerely, to like many things about the United States, but any specific act or policy of its government seems to have exceptional difficulty in meeting with their approval. Moreover, their publicly stated disapproval is not confined to matters of direct concern to their country. For example, at this very juncture they took time off from Argentina's domestic crisis to produce a 30-page pamphlet on Puerto Rico which was strongly biased against the United States.

The Christian Democratic movement in Argentina is represented by two new parties with similar names but of different character, the Christian Democratic Party and the Christian Democratic Federal Union. The former is the more liberal of the two; the latter supported the "Catholic reactionaries" of the Amadeo type in Lonardi's government and was the only party that did not resign from the Consultative Council in the crisis just before Lonardi's fall.[7] The division of Christian Democratic strength between these

[7] For the National Consultative Council, see above, p. 35.

two parties illustrates—as do schisms in the Radical, Socialist, and Communist parties—the tendency to political fragmentation in Argentina, which seems to be growing.

Just how strong these two parties are it is impossible to say, since both are quite new, one having been organized in May 1955 and the other in July. If they could unite, they might develop considerable strength among those liberal and moderately left-wing elements which, though otherwise generally sympathetic towards the traditional aims of the Radical Party, are repelled by its anticlericalism, for while the new parties are not clerical in the sense of being organs of the hierarchy, they are definitely pro-Catholic. They stand for the type of Christian socialism that has developed into so strong a political force in West Germany, France, and Italy since 1945. The encouragement offered by these European precedents seems to have played an important part in generating the Christian Democratic movement in Argentina. The process was delayed, however, by the hierarchy's alliance with Perón in his early years and did not get well under way until the weakened alliance split wide open in November 1954.

The stimulus of the European example was needed, if one were to judge only by the past, for the very few parties of this type that have previously been formed in Argentina (such as the Democratic Christian Union, in 1916) have been small, weak, and short-lived. The present movement may have better prospects. Radical observers naturally take a bearish view of these, on the grounds that there has been no collapse of values in Argentina like the one that has stimulated the political growth of Christian socialism in Europe since 1945; that the Argentine Christian Democrats have not produced a clean-cut program of action; and that in the critical closing months of Perón's regime they showed more zeal for the defense of the Catholic Church than of the

Argentine nation. This reasoning may be persuasive, but it is not convincing to the present writer, who believes that with proper management the Christian Democrats could take advantage of the present revolutionary situation in Argentina to make themselves one of the country's major parties.

Of the two definitely left-wing parties, Socialists and Communists, we shall speak more briefly, for neither has had much weight in Argentina in recent years or seems likely to have much more in the years just ahead. Since its establishment in 1894 the Argentine Socialist Party has had some of Argentina's most noted intellectuals as its leaders, and one of the ablest of all its leaders, Américo Ghioldi, is now back at the helm after a long exile; but its followers have always been too few and have been concentrated geographically in the cities, above all in Buenos Aires, and socially in the labor unions, which in the past decade have been Peronized—how lastingly no one yet knows.

The Socialist Party, too, fell victim to the divisive tactics of Perón, who so recently as 1953 made a convert of no less a person than Enrique Dickmann, former editor of the Socialist newspaper *La Vanguardia* and many times a Socialist deputy in Congress. The anti-Peronista Socialists have now been recognized by the appointment of their "grand old man" Alfredo Palacios as the ambassador of the Provisional Government to democratic Uruguay; but that is the type of public power with which the party will probably have to be content for a long time to come. In the visible future it will be doing well if it becomes again the influential though small minority group that it was when, a half century ago, this same Alfredo Palacios took a leading part in the enactment of Argentina's first workingmen's law.

Estimates of Communist Party membership in Argentina have varied widely in recent years, but within low limits, and the most recent estimate of 80,000 falls within this range. Moreover, Perón first checked the growth of the Communist Party, then succeeded in splitting it, as he did all other opposition groups, and thereafter used the residual factions alternately as henchmen and whipping boys. In the last few years of his regime his democratic critics at home and abroad asserted that it was falling under Communist influence, but the assertion was implausible and the evidence offered in support of it unconvincing. Even if it was true, any advantage gained by the Communists in Perón's later years was lost with his fall; and in post-Perón Argentina one party certainly, and perhaps two, should be able to outbid them for mass support. The first is the majority group of the Radical Party under its new leadership, the second is the now suppressed Peronista Party if it should come to life again. The latter two are firmly rooted in Argentina, whereas Communism under whatever guise bears the made-in-Moscow label. These facts are well known to the Argentine masses, who are about as literate and intelligent as comparable groups in any other country and who also share their fellow countrymen's ardent nationalism so fully that most of them prefer to conduct even the class struggle in nationalistic terms and to achieve social reforms, or social revolution, under an Argentine banner. Only if some unexpected turn of events should wreck the Radical Party would Communism be likely to make great headway in Argentina in the near future.

At the opposite end of the political spectrum are the relatively large National Democratic (commonly called Conservative) Party and the much smaller Progresive Democratic Party (usually abbreviated as P.D.P.). Both have ties with the oligarchy, though both also have considerable support outside it—otherwise they would hardly have achieved even the status of splinter groups.

The leadership of the P.D.P. is competent and courageous —witness the speech made by its spokesman, Dr. Luciano F. Molinas, on August 23, 1955, in response to Perón's peace offensive. This was an exceptionally thoughtful as well as outspoken address and in it Molinas, unlike the Radical and Conservative spokesmen in this crisis, ventured to criticize not only Perón but the armed forces, which, he declared, "exceed the needs of our country and of the international situation . . . Nor can we accept," he continued, with obvious reference to General Lucero's recent public praise of Perón, "that officers and military chiefs perform public acts of adulation to one man."

Nevertheless, the P.D.P. is too small and too closely linked to the original core of the oligarchy, the great landowners, to count for much in a free democratic society such as the Provisional Government promises to re-establish in Argentina. The Peronista speaker who replied to Molinas on August 26 was substantially right when he said:

". . . The Progressive Democratic Party's influence is limited to a small geographic and socioeconomic sphere. . . . [It] has its northern limits at the southern border of Santa Fe Province and [extends south through Entre Ríos and] part of northern Buenos Aires Province and is socially and economically confined to landowners who have held sway over the vast agricultural and ranching area . . . The party's influence also extends to the less prominent, though financially well-to-do, ranchers and farmers in the southern-most areas."

Uniting these elements with "influential bankers" and "the great foreign monopolies which owned the packing houses," he continued, the P.D.P. was a main prop of the old "feudal" era and devoted itself mainly to getting "ever higher prices" for farm and ranch products. The picture was overdrawn, but there was so much truth in it that the P.D.P., which was never a major party in the past, can hardly hope to become one in the future under any conceivable successor to the Perón regime. It might, however, gain a modest share of public power by entering into a coalition with its cousins, the Conservatives, and other like-minded elements.

The Conservative Party is not only much larger than the P.D.P., but also more broadly representative. Its membership has long been drawn from the middle as well as the upper class and from certain urban as well as rural groups, for it has appealed to all those who are of a conservative bent whether for social, cultural, religious, or economic reasons. In recent years its appeal has been particularly strong to devout Catholics,[8] who, politically speaking, had nowhere else to go until the rise of the Christian Democratic movement in 1955, since Radicals, Socialists, Communists, and, more recently, Peronistas have been decidely anticlerical. In times past the Conservatives were also able to dragoon large numbers of the rural and urban workers into supporting them at the polls, but the Electoral Reform Law of 1912 (the Sáenz Peña Law) and other changes have put a stop to this practice. As a result, the Conservatives, who controlled the national government most of the time before 1916, have never done so since then except through an alliance (*Concordancia*) with a schismatic right-wing Radical group (the Anti-Personalists) from 1932 to 1943.

The Conservatives' conduct in the latter period thoroughly discredited their leadership and led to their overthrow by the military dictatorship of 1943 which in turn produced the Perón regime. Under the latter they did little to rehabilitate their party's reputation, leaving the brunt of the political fight to the Radicals. Since they did not present a ticket in the only recent national election (1951), but

[8] Note for example the Conservative spokesman Vicente Solano Lima's reply to Perón's pacification plea, above, pp. 14–15.

merely supported the Radical ticket, there is no adequate basis for a close estimate of their voting strength, but this is probably well below that of the Peronistas (if they were permitted to vote) and the Radicals, though far above that of the Socialists and still farther above the Communists'.

Nevertheless, their social and economic strength makes the Conservatives a political factor of first-rate importance under such a regime as the Provisional Government and in the present atmosphere of widespread reaction against the demagoguery that characterized the Perón regime, especially in its last frantic weeks. As for the next stage, while almost anything short of a Communist victory might come out of the present confusion, it is at least not unthinkable that one solution might be another *Concordancia* somewhat like the one that followed the military dictatorship of 1930-1931 —an alliance of Conservatives with some other political group or groups, tacitly backed by the armed forces. Such a coalition would naturally include the P.D.P., but it would be most likely to succeed if it also again included right-wing Radicals, as did the *Concordancia* of the 1930s.

Much will therefore depend upon whether the new Radical leadership is more successful in uniting the party than it has been at any time since the mid 1920s.[9] If it succeeds in this, it will probably be able to prevent another coalition of conservative groups from ruling Argentina, at any rate with any pretense of democracy. But what then? At present, the Radicals probably do not have the votes to win a national election by themselves and their majority bloc is opposed on principle to coalitions. They might turn the trick by making converts of now partyless Peronistas, but on the other hand, as we have already suggested, such conversions on the left could lead to defections from the

[9] See above, pp. 48–49, for the warning sounded on Nov. 3, 1955, by Radical leader Sammartino.

Radical Party's right wing, leaving little if any net gain.

It is quite possible that no party or firm coalition of parties will command a majority in Argentina for some time to come and that she will be plagued, as her next-door neighbor Chile and France have long been, by a multiple-party system. The outlook in Argentina for political stability under a democratic regime is not very promising, at least in the near future.

PART III

International relations

1. Introduction

The following discussion of the international significance of the recent upheaval in Argentina has been prepared with an eye to the whole range of that country's foreign relations, both by countries and by categories. Nevertheless, since we must be selective, the stress will be laid here upon Argentine relations with the United States and upon the political and economic aspects of Argentine foreign relations at large. This emphasis can be justified on the grounds that since World War II the United States has become the most important foreign nation in the world to Argentina (a position previously held by Great Britain for more than a century) and that in the case of Argentina the closely related political and economic aspects of foreign affairs provide a serviceable focus for all the rest. The following discussion will of course include both bilateral and multilateral relations and will stress the continuity of the preference that Argentine governments of whatever kind have traditionally shown for arrangements of the former type, especially in matters relating to security.

There are several reasons why the Argentine upheaval possesses considerable international significance, particularly from the point of view of the United States. In the first place, there is the importance of Argentina in the international scale, which is sufficient to lend interest to any change in its government that affects its international role. To be sure, Argentina not only ranks far below the great powers but also hardly ranks as high as such "middle" powers as The Netherlands, Canada, and Australia in either economic development or military strength. On the other hand, politically Argentina outweighs any of the middle powers because she holds a position not occupied by any of them: that of a leading member in a well-defined group of nations. The group to which Argentina belongs is of course the one made up of the twenty Latin American states, which, for all their diversity and internal differences, have acted as a bloc with increasing frequency in the past dozen years. A symbol of their growing unity is their decision, announced in October 1955, to erect on United Nations Plaza in New York City a club building for their delegates to the United Nations. Moreover, as the third Latin American nation in population and the first in economic and cultural development, Argentina has been a major factor in the Inter-American System (now the Organization of American States) throughout the present century, and a not inconsiderable factor in the old League of Nations in the 1930s and, since 1945, in the United Nations. In international trade, Argentina's position in the Latin American family is outstanding, for she accounts for more than one fifth of the total export and import trade of these twenty nations.

These facts are of special interest from the point of view of the United States, which since 1914 has successively supplanted Great Britain as the Number One nation first in Argentina's import trade, then investments in Argentina, and finally in her export trade. Though larger than those of any other nation, the investments of the United States in Argentina (currently estimated at about $400 million) are small in comparison with its investments in several other countries, but they were held down by Perón's policies and would probably expand greatly in a more favorable atmosphere. One of the big question marks about post-Perón Argentina is whether it will create such an atmosphere.

Politically, too, Argentina's importance to the United States has increased greatly in recent decades. Unfortunately, the relations between the two countries during this period have been characterized most of the time by antagonism over one issue or another. This reached its height in the Perón period, but it had already become dangerous under the Conservative regime which he helped to overthrow in 1943, and had frequently been sharp under the preceding Radical regime from 1916 to 1930. Consequently, when in his last two years Perón veered around and made the development of better relations with the United States a major objective of his foreign policy, he was going against the trend of the past four decades.

As we shall see, Perón's enemies made his rapprochement with the United States—or, perhaps one should say, the form which the rapprochement took—a major point of attack on his regime in the last months of its life. This fact lends special interest to the question: What foreign policy will post-Perón Argentina follow? Will it continue the type of cooperation with the United States that helped to unhorse him? Or will it find other types of cooperation with the United States that are more agreeable to the Argentine people? Or will it try to revive the balance-of-power policy followed by Perón before 1953 and by many of his predecessors—the policy of playing off the United States against one or more European powers, such as Britain, Germany, Italy, and the Soviet Union? The answers to these questions will also provide the answer to a related and broader question: Will the new regime continue the half-hearted internationalism of Perón, or make it whole-hearted, or, following another of the leads provided by Perón's opportunistic and confused foreign policy, will it revert to the quasi-isolationism of the first Radical president, Hipólito Irigoyen?

2. Perón's foreign policy under fire

Before we discuss the assault on Perón's foreign policy in 1955, let us review briefly the major features of his policy down to that time.

Except that it was strongly nationalistic (two of the three stated major objectives of the Perón regime were the defense of Argentina's political sovereignty and the establishment of her economic independence), Perón's foreign policy had no guiding principle save his vaunted Third Position, or middle way, between Communism and capitalism, between Moscow and Washington. Even this principle, which was tacitly abandoned after 1953, did not serve as a guiding one in the pinches before that date. It did serve as a vote-catching device at home, and that seems to have been one of its two major purposes, the other being diplomatic bargaining or blackmail. But whenever a showdown seemed at hand in the cold war, he sided with the United States (as in the crisis of June 1950 over Korea), only to resume his Yankeephobe tactics as soon as the danger passed.

For various reasons, there were likewise sweeping changes in his relations with other powers that do not seem to be susceptible of explanation in terms of any basic policy, but which reflected sheer opportunism. A case in point is that of Franco Spain, which at first was his close friend when it was his only one, but towards which he cooled after 1948, when his position seemed stronger. Likewise, while professing loyalty to Argentina's traditional policy of bilateral alliances, he committed his country to multilateral arrangements and then failed to carry these out in good faith. As a member of the Organization of American States, his government ratified the Rio Defense Treaty of 1947 but not the Bogotá Charter of 1948, and although it was an active member of the United Nations, it did not join Unesco, the International Bank for Reconstruction and Development (World Bank), or the International Monetary Fund.

In regard to Latin America, and more particularly the River Plate area, which Argentines have long regarded as their proper sphere of influence, he followed a somewhat more settled course aimed at promoting the hegemony of Argentina. Even in this case, however, there were such wide variations in the means employed—which ranged from threats and revolutionary intrigues to proposals for economic union and efforts at persuasion through the use of labor attachés to spread the Peronista doctrine—that these represented so many changes in basic policy. In the case of the most important country of all, big Brazil, Perón's attitude was ambivalent: at times it reflected the traditional rivalry between the two countries, which has long been a major factor in South American power politics, while at other times it suggested that Perón hoped for some cooperative arrangement through the influence of his Brazilian counterpart, Getulio Vargas, from whose dictatorship in 1937–1945 Perón had derived some useful hints for his own regime. Vargas' re-election in 1952 is said to have been aided by Perón, but any hopes the latter may have conceived on this account were not fulfilled and they were blasted by Vargas' suicide midway in his term—an event which in retrospect appears to have been one of the first tremors of the earthquake that was to shatter Perón's regime.

The changes in Perón's South American policy may have represented an effort at adjustment to a deteriorating situation, for his experience with Brazil was matched by similar disappointments at the same time with regard to Chile and Bolivia, both of which preferred cooperation with the United States to Perón's embrace. As a result, by 1955 his government's sphere of influence was confined to adjacent Paraguay, the smallest, poorest, and weakest state in South America. On the other hand, neighboring Uruguay, which had steadfastly resisted his influence, continued to serve as an asylum for refugees from his tyranny and as a base for their efforts to overthrow him.

The fiasco of Perón's bid for hegemony, which failed not only in Latin America at large but even in the restricted River Plate area, probably contributed to his abandonment of the Third Position in favor of a rapprochement with the very power which he had so often denounced as the spearhead of capitalist-imperialism, the United States. This diplomatic revolution was never announced or admitted by him, but it was apparent both in the new tone of cordiality that marked his references to the government at Washington after the visit paid him in 1953 by Milton S. Eisenhower, brother of the President, and also in concrete acts, such as his acceptance of a $60 million Export-Import Bank loan for the construction of a steel plant in Argentina and the negotiation of the contract with the Standard Oil Company of California subsidiary, to which reference has already been made. Rumors of even more important developments along this line, including military cooperation with the United States, were encouraged by the visits of businessmen, Congressmen, and military officials from the United States to Argentina, and by the cordial reception they apparently received from the authorities in that country.

The result was a strong and rising wave of protest in Argentina, where both anti-imperialism and Yankeephobia have been deeply rooted since the turn of the century. With the rise of the United States to world power, these two themes have been merged into one. Perón himself had formerly worn it threadbare, and now he had put himself in a position where his own words could be turned against him.

The opposition leaders lost no time in making the most of the golden opportunity afforded them by his tergiversation. The Radicals, the largest and traditionally the most nationalistic and anti-imperialistic of Argentina's opposition parties, appropriately headed the assault. The passage on this subject in their spokesman Frondizi's radio address on July 28, 1955, which has already been cited in another connection,[1] was comparatively mild:

> "In the field of international policy [said Frondizi], the country cannot continue on a vacillating road, which places it alternately at the mercy of one or another imperialist. We cannot continue to postpone the solution of serious international problems on the ground that another world war may break out. The Argentine nation should follow an independent national policy, specifically and positively its own, based on an understanding of the political sovereignty of the country, as well as on the economic and social sovereignty of the people.
>
> "It is necessary to maintain these three types of sovereignty and on them to build an international policy which would strengthen the brotherhood of our American countries and would place Argentina in the position of a country in the service of democracy and the brotherhood of the nations of the world, and of mankind in general."

[1] See above, pp. 12–13.

The speaker was doubtless sincere in what he said about strengthening "the brotherhood of our American countries" and putting Argentina at the service of "the brotherhood of the nations of the world," but as soon as we pass from the generalities of this speech to the positions taken by the Radicals on concrete issues during this critical period, we are struck by their animus against the largest of the American countries and by their failure to make any substantial distinction between the cause of the Communist world and that of the free world.

The touchstone of this period is the contract, already frequently mentioned,[2] between the Perón government and a subsidiary of the Standard Oil Company of California for the exploration and exploitation of oil lands in Patagonia (southern Argentina). The announcement that some such agreement had been concluded was made on March 29, 1955, and on May 10 the contract was submitted to Congress for its approval. On the latter date the National Committee of the Radical Party issued a four-page mimeographed statement, signed by Arturo Frondizi as chairman, which brought together in one package this oil contract and several other issues, including those relating to the Falkland Islands, the Antarctic, the economic and military penetration of Argentina by the United States, and even Perón's anticlerical campaign.[3]

This Radical statement was in the main a blast against Yankee imperialism and against Perón for his alleged surrender (*entrega*) of Argentina to it. Great Britain and the International Court of Justice also came in for their share

[2] See above, pp. 13, 36, 99.
[3] Entitled "En defensa de la soberanía argentina en el sud del continente" and dated Buenos Aires, May 10, 1955, this document is captioned "Unión Cívica Radical, Comité Nacional, Río Bamba 482" and is signed by the committee's secretary, Federico Monjardín, as well as its chairman (*presidente*), Arturo Frondizi.

of castigation but this was administered on the clearly
implied ground that they were aiding in the sacrifice of
Argentina to Yankee imperialism.

The statement was divided into four sections. The first
of these, which was largely expository, dealt with the
recently announced decision of the governments of Argentina and Chile to arbitrate a boundary question relating to
the Beagle Channel of the Strait of Magellan.

The fireworks began in the second section. Here the
projected arbitration was denounced on the ground that the
territory in question was indisputably Argentine and hence
as unsuitable a subject for arbitration as other Argentine
territories in that part of the world, including the Falkland
Islands, South Georgia, and the Argentine sector of Antarctica. The reader was then reminded that in 1942 the United
States had tried to get permission to establish air and naval
bases in the Strait of Magellan, and it was clearly implied
that the projected arbitration was being undertaken as part
of a gigantic plan to extend the military and industrial
influence of the United States over Argentina proper as
well as the Strait of Magellan and the Antarctic. "It is easy
to see," the statement continued, "that the installation of
certain industrial plants of the United States in our territory
[the new Kaiser plant at Córdoba had just been mentioned]
and the oil contract now in negotiation do not have a merely
economic purpose but that they have a well defined
strategic significance as well, which conforms to plans drawn
up by the United States Chiefs of Staff . . . [and that
these] are aimed at the installation of naval and military
bases in our southern territory." In this connection it was
also asserted that the current religious controversy in Argentina had been "artificially created" by Perón as a smoke
screen to hide the steps he was taking to aid the United
States in its designs.

The theme was further developed in the third section, appropriately entitled "Our sovereignty in the Antarctic and the pretensions of the United States." Here it was asserted that "while the great powers are interested in the incalculable wealth of the Antarctic in minerals, hunting, and fishing, their major preoccupation at present is with the strategic necessity of assuring themselves of the rich uranium resources of the Antarctic and of installing powerful naval and military bases there for defense and attack in case of another great war." If, the statement continued, "the sector theory" applied in the Arctic were established with regard to the Antarctic, as Argentina insists, the latter would possess sovereignty over the area between 25° and 74° west longitude; but the application of the "sector theory" to the Antarctic [4] is threatened by the refusal of the United States either to recognize or to assert territorial claims in this region. Commenting on the recent news that the United States was about to send "an extraordinary exploring expedition" to the Antarctic, the statement observed: "The true purposes [of this expedition] are not hidden. It is admitted that naval-military bases will be installed, and it is easy to conjecture that atomic experiments will be conducted [there]." [5]

[4] For the background, see David Winston Herron, "Antarctic Claims," *Foreign Affairs*, Vol. 32, No. 4 (July, 1954), pp. 661–667, in which the "Polar Sector" rule, first proposed in 1907, is described as "an arbitrary device, reminiscent of Alexander VI's Papal Bull of 1493 dividing the globe between Spain and Portugal," and in which, with reference to the inclusion of "the American Quadrant of the Antarctic in [the] mutual defense area" covered by the Rio Treaty, the ambiguous statement is made that "this treaty, in effect, applied the Monroe Doctrine to the Antarctic for the first time."
[5] The Radicals did not exaggerate the importance of this expedition, which is referred to in the United States as "Operation Deepfreeze." When the first ship, an icebreaker described as "one of the most powerful in the world," sailed from the United States for the Antarctic on November 2, 1955, it was publicly described as "the vanguard of an historic expedition" by Rear Admiral Richard E. Byrd, who had just been placed in charge of all the United States' activities in the Antarctic. Byrd's statement mentioned only the sci-

In the fourth section the actions of Great Britain in submitting the Falkland Islands dispute to the International Court of Justice, and of the latter in agreeing to consider the case, were sharply criticized on the ground that Argentina's consent, which was necessary, had not been given. That this consent should not be given was asserted in the title of this section: "Argentina ought not to agree to arbitration with regard to its territories in the Antarctic."

The document concluded with an unnumbered section summarizing the Radical Party's position on the points discussed above. The United States was not mentioned by name again but it was clearly alluded to in the references made to "foreign nations" for whose benefit the "economic surrender" and the "concession of naval and military bases" were being made by the Perón regime.

Shortly after this the Radical Party issued another blast addressed primarily to the Argentine youth, concentrated against the projected contract with the Standard Oil Company of California, and mockingly entitled "The Anti-Imperialism of the [Perón] Regime." [6] What is at stake here, it was asserted, is nothing less than the national patrimony of Argentina, for if this contract should go through, "foreign capitalists would become the economic masters of Argentina, the door would be opened to the installation of strategic bases in our territory," and we should become "a true colony of exploitation, a chicken to whom one sells its own

---

entific aspect of the expedition, but his directive from the government, issued by the Defense Department, made it one of his duties to act as adviser to the Operations Coordinating Board of the National Security Council. Statements by "Navy spokesmen" and an "official spokesman" indicated that one purpose was to establish permanent bases, thus placing the United States "on the same footing as Chile, Argentina, Great Britain, and Australia" in the Antarctic. (New York Times, Nov. 3, 1955.)

[6] One page, mimeographed, endorsed "No. 2, Informativo de Política, Oficina Universitaria de la Unión Cívica Radical." Undated but signed after May 10, 1955.

eggs." Not even the old oligarchy at its worst would have dreamed of making such a surrender and "the most elementary sense of patriotism requires us to resist the sale of our country to foreign imperialism."

Whether or not the terms of the contract were in fact disadvantageous to Argentina is a question on which the present writer, who has no expert knowledge of the subject, would not venture an opinion. What is certain, however, is that the issue was a godsend to the Radicals and the other enemies of Perón. So unpopular was the contract that the Peronista Party itself was deeply divided over it and did not take an official position in favor of the contract until the very eve of the final revolt, despite the fact that it had been submitted to Congress on May 10 and the deadline for its ratification by that body was September 30, after which it would by its terms lapse if not so ratified. In a belated effort to stem the tide of opposition the government had no less a person than the Minister of Industry, Orlando L. Santos, defend the contract in a long and carefully prepared address on August 25 to a select "live" audience as well as a radio audience, and the speech was rebroadcast the next day. At last on September 15 a spokesman for the Superior Council of the Peronista Party also defended the contract in a long address; but this came far too late to do Perón any good, for the revolt that ousted him began the following day.

Of the two conservative parties, only the Progressive Democratic Party had much to say about foreign policy in reply to Perón's appeal for pacification. The National Democratic (Conservative) Party's reply, broadcast on August 10, dealt wholly with domestic issues except in its protest against Perón's anticlerical policy and "the materialistic tendencies of extreme leftist ideologies" which this encouraged.

On the other hand, the Progressive Democratic Party's rejoinder to Perón, broadcast on August 23, gave his foreign policy a thorough going over. It branded his projected oil contract as an "outrageous" concession to foreign interests, ridiculed his whole foreign policy as "vacillating and confused," and denounced his failure to protest the "invasion" of Guatemala in June 1954 "in defiance of the public indignation of all America." The latter phrase involved a great exaggeration, but the significant thing about this passage is that it was another thrust at the United States, for the "invasion" in quesion, which overthrew the communist-infected Arbenz government of Guatemala, had the blessing of Washington. Ironically in view of subsequent events, Perón was also criticized by the P.D.P. spokesman on the ground that when the right of asylum was discussed in international conferences, his delegates had always "voted against the dispositions which guarantee political exiles the free expression of their opinion."

These examples could be multiplied, but enough have been given to show that in the months just before Perón's overthrow the opposition to him was based in considerable measure on his foreign policy, and that the most criticized features of his foreign policy were his failure to protect the national interests of Argentina and, related to this, his economic and military cooperation with the United States. One must, of course, discount the nationalism and Yankee-phobia of these attacks somewhat in recognition of the fact that they were the talking points of an opposition which had to avail itself of any issue that would help to undermine a tyrant. On the other hand, it must also be recognized that these particular issues of nationalism and Yankeephobia would have been worth little or nothing as talking points if they had not aroused a favorable response among many Argentines, and that his opponents would not have laid so much stress on them if they had not been confident that such a response would be forthcoming. The real test, of course, would come when the post-Perón government of Argentina formulated its own foreign policy.

3. Lonardi's foreign policy beginnings

The Provisional Government's foreign policy has not taken definite shape at the present writing (December 1, 1955), but the process has gone far enough to indicate the major lines along which it will probably develop. These may, of course, be altered under pressure of circumstances as the situation changes and it should be remembered that whatever policy the present government adopts will in a sense be provisional, like the government itself. Nevertheless, the decisions so far taken are likely to limit future choices in some degree, as is usually the case with the first decisions of any new regime.

First let us look at the foreign policy of Lonardi, under whom all the significant developments to date have taken place. This revealed the following major features: (1) In important respects it exhibited strongly nationalistic tendencies in response to political and economic pressures which are not likely to relax in the near future. (2) The anti-colonialism and "Spanish Americanism" of preceding administrations—including Perón's most of the time—were maintained, though perhaps in a somewhat attenuated form. (3) Within the not too broad limits thus set, Lonardi's government sought to maintain friendly relations with the United States and to make Argentina a more cooperative member of the Organization of American States. (4) There was no substantial alteration of Perón's mixed policy towards the United Nations, which combined active participation in the parent body with abstention from most of its specialized organizations.

These general features will become clearer if we examine the relevant personnel of the new government and certain specific issues with which it has had to deal.

With regard to personnel, the first thing to note is that the Lonardi government's minister of foreign affairs, Mario Amadeo, was a nationalist, a Yankeephobe, an advocate of Latin American as against Pan American cooperation, and a former associate of Perón's in the military dictatorship set up in 1943, from which he resigned in 1945 in protest against the break with Hitler's Germany. Amadeo's appointment as Minister of Foreign Affairs came as a shock to most well-wishers of the Lonardi government in the United States.

An appointment of a different kind, but of even greater importance, was that of Raúl Prebisch as special economic consultant to the new regime. An able financier and economist and former manager of the Argentine Central Bank, Prebisch opposed Perón and went into exile. Since 1948 he has headed and dominated the increasingly influential United Nations Economic Commission for Latin America (ECLA), which was established in that year. Early in October 1955 Prebisch was brought back to Argentina, on leave from ECLA, to examine the economic wreckage of the Perón regime and recommend a new economic policy to the government. He was soon given the title of financial and economic adviser to the President.

In view of the character of the Argentine economy, this appointment was likely to have great international significance. The prospect opened up by it was disturbing from Washington's point of view, partly because Prebisch was an advocate of extensive government intervention in economic affairs and to that extent an opponent of the free enterprise system preached by Washington, and also because, as head of ECLA, he was thoroughly committed to the thesis that the more advanced countries (meaning principally the United States) could and should aid in the development of less advanced countries through government-to-government investments—a thesis which ran counter to Washington's thesis that such aid should normally be provided only by private investments. Moreover, Simon Hanson, an expert in this field, has warned: "With reference to Argentine trade with the United States, ECLA has pointed to a return to the principle of 'buy from those who buy from us,' with which the United States business community was flayed during the 30s in the [River] Plate [area]." Hanson notes that the State Department cited Prebisch's Argentine appointment "as one more proof that its position of upholding Perón had been sound."[7] The main question is how far Prebisch and the new Argentine government will go in putting into practice the theories which he has developed in ECLA.

Turning from personnel problems to specific issues of foreign policy, we may appropriately begin with the oil question, which helped to bring about Perón's downfall.[8] In his very first public pronouncement, a "Proclamation of Freedom" delivered at the beginning of the revolt on September 16, General Lonardi made an indirect reference to the nub of this issue, the pending contract with a Standard Oil of California subsidiary, and indicated his stand on it, by denouncing the Perón regime as one which "endangers the future of the Republic through the surrender of its sources of wealth." A week later, having triumphed and in-

[7] This whole subject is discussed in *Hanson's Latin American Letter,* No. 551, Washington, October 8, 1955.
[8] See above, pp. 104–106.

stalled his government in Buenos Aires, he said of the "pact on petroleum" that "according to authoritative sources, including foreign ones, [it] is not advantageous to us," and continued: "I will do whatever is necessary to acquire the technical equipment required for us to drill on our own." As expected, he let the contract lapse on September 30.

Lonardi's alternative solution of the oil problem was forthcoming almost at once. This was to substitute for the Standard of California subsidiary an Argentine government organization, the Y.P.F.,[9] which has had nearly twenty years' experience in this field, and to depend, as far as possible, on Argentine rather than foreign capital in financing the extensive prospecting, drilling, and refining operations in view. "The Provisional Government," General Lonardi told a reporter on October 3, "will attach special importance to the exploitation of petroleum. It will seek ways of getting the participation of Argentine capital that is willing to cooperate." That same afternoon he presided at the installation of the new general administrator of the Y.P.F., who, incidentally, was a retired Army general, and the government set about rehabilitating that organization, which Perón was charged with having sabotaged for the benefit of foreign oil companies.

It remains to be seen whether this solution of the oil problem is feasible, but there can be no question that some solution is urgently needed, for about half of Argentina's large and growing petroleum requirements have to be met by imports from abroad and this absorbs so large a part of Argentina's available foreign exchange that not enough remains to finance other imports needed to keep the country's economy operating at the current level, much less to develop

[9] Y.P.F. stands for Yacimientos Petrolíferos Argentinos, which since 1936 has had a monopoly of the Argentine oil industry, with the important exception that private companies previously established (1915–1936) in Argentina have been permitted to continue to operate there.

it further. In many respects—including the magnitude of the problem and the strength of national resistance to solving it by accepting "foreign exploitation"—Argentina's oil problem resembles the one which in the past few years has brought Brazil into a state of serious economic and political instability. There are differences, of course, and one of the most important is that Argentina has the experienced Y.P.F., which by this time should certainly have built up a large back-log of technical and managerial skill, and for which Brazil has no counterpart.[10] No matter how well Y.P.F. does its part of the job, however, great difficulties regarding capital and foreign exchange will still remain to be overcome. Prebisch's ECLA recently proposed a solution for them, but this has been judged utterly unrealistic by the authority cited above, Simon Hanson, who concludes that: "Working in a vacuum [i.e., the vacuum of ECLA] clearly permits a freedom of imagination that will be lacking if the head of ECLA assumes the practical task of writing policy for Argentina."

Two conclusions about Argentina's thorny and crucially important oil problem seem warranted. The first is that it would not be politically feasible for any Argentine government in the near future to entrust the solution of this problem to foreign private enterprise, least of all to a United States private corporation or its subsidiary, as Perón tried to do. The second is that if the alternative solution chosen by Lonardi does not succeed, as seems quite possible, Argentina will suffer from instability and recurring crises, in its foreign relations as well as its domestic politics, as Brazil has done, until a better solution is found. Still another solution might be provided now by the United States in the form of government-to-government aid, as was suggested in a televised

[10] Brazil does have a similar organization, called Petrobras, but this is no real counterpart since it is quite new and its scale of operations has been much smaller than Y.P.F.'s.

broadcast by General Lonardi to the United States late in October. This situation raises a difficult and highly important question of United States foreign policy which will be considered in the following section.

Insofar as good will and fair words are concerned, the United States could hardly ask for more than General Lonardi gave it. At his first full press conference on September 28, which lasted only fifteen minutes, he took time to underline his desire for closer relations with the United States and to say that he was not thinking of economic aid alone. "The great nation to the north," he continued, "is making great spiritual progress. It gives me pleasure to say that [when I was in the United States] I was deeply impressed by social conditions there."

Lonardi subsequently maintained the same attitude even on the touchy subject of U.S. private investments in Argentina, declaring that in general these would be welcomed by his government and that he had opposed the Standard Oil contract only because of the special issues involved. So far as is known, no new test case has yet arisen, but for what it is worth we may note the evidence provided by the case of the Kaiser Motors enterprise at Córdoba, which was not molested by Lonardi despite the fact that it was launched in close cooperation with the Perón regime. The value of this evidence may be questioned, for Hanson believes that it reflects good will towards the Kaiser enterprise not on the part of the Lonardi government but of Washington. When the former supplanted Perón, he asserts, the State Department rushed to "defend the Kaiser investment with the shield of the Exim Bank steel loan," that is, the Export-Import Bank's $60 million loan for a steel mill which was on the point of being made to Perón when he fell and which Lonardi's government wished to inherit.[11]

[11] *Hanson's Latin American Letter,* No. 550, Washington, October 1, 1955.

For obvious reasons, Argentina's attitude towards the Inter-American System at any given time has usually been closely related to her attitude towards the United States. Perón's spotty record in this respect has already been noted. Lonardi's record began auspiciously with the announcement that Argentina would "very soon" ratify the Charter of the Organization of American States, which Perón's government had helped to draw up at the Bogotá Inter-American Conference of 1948, and had signed, but had never ratified.

This announcement was made on October 11 by none other than formerly anti-Pan American Foreign Minister Amadeo in the course of an important interview. He appropriately coupled it with the statement that his government wished to cultivate particularly close "political and spiritual" cooperation with the United States. "My hope," said Amadeo, "is that when I leave this office these relations [with the United States] will be better than ever."

Ratifying the Bogotá Charter would be a gesture in that sense, but it is not easy to see that it would make much political difference in Argentina's participation in the activities of the OAS, for nonratification has not prevented Argentina from participating in these freely and fully ever since 1948—in permanent bodies such as the OAS Council or governing board as well as in special meetings, such as that of the American Ministers of Foreign Affairs at Washington in 1951, the Tenth Inter-American Conference at Caracas early in 1954, and the conference of American Ministers of Finance at Rio de Janeiro late in the same year.

Moreover, Amadeo did not clarify his government's attitude towards the Rio Defense Treaty of 1947, which has been a highly controversial subject in Argentina from the start, but which Washington, because of the cold war, has regarded as considerably more important than the Bogotá Charter. In order to put teeth into the treaty, the United

States has negotiated a series of bilateral military pacts with several other Latin American countries, but not with Argentina. When the important question whether the Lonardi government would enter into such a pact was put to Amadeo in the interview of October 11 mentioned above, he replied noncommittally that the subject was under study.

On two issues relating to the southern reaches of the hemisphere, the new government made its position quite clear, and in both cases this was substantially identical with the stand taken by Perón. It would not agree to the adjudication of the long-standing Falkland Islands dispute with Great Britain by the International Court of Justice, and it would maintain Argentina's claim to a slice of Antarctica.

In his policy pronouncement of October 11 Amadeo also spoke more broadly of Argentina's international role. Laying the ghost of Perón's Third Position (which had been moribund if not dead for two years), he said that on global issues Argentina would abjure neutralism and stand squarely with the Western Nations, "because," he explained, "we have an affinity to the West as a result of our common heritage of Christian civilization." With reference to a specific and burning issue of global scope, anti-colonialism, he declared that his government would abandon the settled anti-colonial policy of Perón and would henceforth act according to the merits of each case.

In practice, however, there was no great change from the later Perón period in this respect, at least as regarded co-operation with the United States. For example, when on September 30 the UN General Assembly voted to discuss the question of Algeria, thereby provoking the withdrawal of the French delegation from the Assembly, Argentina voted as usual with the anti-colonial powers and was on the opposite side from the United States. That was shortly before Amadeo made the important policy pronouncement which we have been discussing. After it was made, however, Argentina still went its own way, which was still different from that of the United States and, on this occasion, from that of the great majority of Latin American states as well. Thus, on October 19 the United States moved that the Assembly shelve the deadlocked election to the Security Council and proceed with elections to the Economic Council and the Trusteeship Council; the motion was opposed by the Soviet Union and carried only by a narrow majority; most of the other Latin American countries voted for it, but Argentina abstained.

Argentina's relations with her South American neighbors were dominated in the first month after Perón's fall by a dispute with Paraguay over the right of asylum as applied to the case of Perón himself. The Lonardi government did not question the right of asylum and in fact had no ground for doing so since this right, though not recognized in general international law, has long been established in the relations of the Latin American nations, including Argentina, with one another, and is moreover stipulated in an existing treaty between Argentina and Paraguay. Nor could it be denied that Perón was entitled to this right, since he had been personally escorted by the Paraguayan ambassador in Buenos Aires to a Paraguayan gunboat in the city's harbor. On the other hand, there are differences of opinion among Latin Americans regarding the obligations of the country in which asylum is taken. It was this aspect of the question that Lonardi's government chose to argue with Paraguay and it contended for an interpretation that would place the maximum limitations on Perón's freedom of action in that country. This was precisely what Perón had tried to do with regard to Argentine refugees in neighboring countries when he was in power. At that time his opponents had denounced this as persecution; now that they were in power they quite naturally gave him a dose of his own medicine.

The controversy with Paraguay developed in two stages. The first extended from Perón's fall to his arrival in Paraguay some two weeks later. During this period the Lonardi government had the upper hand because the Paraguayan gunboat on which Perón had taken refuge could not leave Buenos Aires without the permission of the port authorities. Apparently (the full story has not been officially revealed) Lonardi used this situation to obtain categorical assurances that the Paraguayan government would not let Perón engage in political activities of any kind. This done, he was permitted to go to Paraguay. He did not make the trip by gunboat after all, but in an amphibious Paraguayan plane to which the gunboat transferred him three miles offshore from Buenos Aires. On his arrival at the capital of Paraguay, Asunción, he was warmly welcomed by his great and good friend, the President of that country.

The second stage began with an interview that Perón gave shortly after his arrival in Paraguay and in which he claimed that he was still the rightful president of Argentina, on the ground that his so-called resignation of September 19 had been only an offer to resign under certain conditions and that these had never been met. The government of Argentina now assumed a publicly threatening tone towards its much weaker neighbor, asserting that the interview constituted a political activity in violation of the terms agreed to by Paraguay, and warning that it would regard the long continuance of Perón's residence in that country as an unfriendly act on the latter's part.

The Paraguayan government hastened to make amends, first by announcing that it would expel Perón if he violated the conditions of his asylum and then by interning him in the very small city of Villarica, in southeastern Paraguay. Ironically, it was on October 17—the anniversary of his great triumph in 1945–that Perón was transferred to his place of internment.[12]

The Lonardi government's relations with Brazil and Chile were featured by efforts to expose Peronista infiltration and intrigue in those countries with the aid of evidence uncovered by the upheaval in Argentina. The initiative in these efforts seems to have come largely from Brazil and Chile and to have been due in some measure to domestic politics and specifically to the desire of certain elements in each country to discredit their rivals by associating them with the fallen Perón. In the magnanimous mood that characterized Lonardi's regime just after his victory, he deprecated these efforts, declaring that it was better to look to the future than the past; but he did not withhold his cooperation.

The only conspicuous result to date is one that may have an important bearing on Argentina's relations with Brazil for some years to come. This was the publication of evidence that an intrigue with Perón had been carried on as far back as 1952 by one of the leading figures in Brazilian public life, João Goulart, vice presidential candidate on the ticket of the bloc that won control of Brazil for the next four years in the national election of October 3, 1955. The presidential candidate on the winning ticket, Juscelino Kubitschek,

[12] On November 2, Perón left Paraguay by plane, reportedly for Nicaragua, but he stopped in Panama and is still there at the present writing. His departure from Paraguay, which was sudden, has been explained in various ways. He asserted that he left of his own volition and in order to relieve Paraguay of the embarrassment of his presence there. One explanation given by his enemies is that he had already caused the Paraguayan government fresh embarrassment and it had retaliated by provoking a fracas near his residence that frightened him into leaving the country post-haste. The embarrassment in question was said to have been caused by a semi-public speech in which Perón asserted that in times past Argentina had seized territory belonging to Paraguay and that he would right this wrong as soon as he returned to power in Buenos Aires. Influential Paraguayans, the story continues, knew that such language would irritate the actual Argentine government and might lead to reprisals against their own country, and so decided to get rid of their dangerous guest.

headed a businessmen's party, but the dynamic Goulart was commonly regarded as the political heir of Getulio Vargas, whose political kinship to Perón we have already noted. The chief item of evidence was a letter allegedly written by Goulart in 1953 regarding a shipment of arms to be made by Perón to Brazil for use by "workers' shock brigades" formed out of the Brazilian equivalent of Perón's descamisados. This letter came to light in Argentina after Perón's fall and an investigation facilitated by the new government there indicated that it was genuine, though some doubt about its authenticity was justified by the fact that it was published by Goulart's political enemies in Brazil on the eve of the election of October 3.

If the final verdict were in favor of the authenticity of the letter, the Brazilian Army officers might carry out the threat which some of them had already made to take over the government by force rather than permit the Kubitschek-Goulart party to gain control of it, for the Brazilian Army has no more liking for descamisado shock brigades than does the Argentine Army. If the threat should be carried out, Brazil would probably have a regime similar to the Provisional Government in Argentina, and this political kinship would augur well for friendly relations between the two countries in the near future, though nothing is likely to eradicate the long-standing rivalry between them, which has often been specifically a rivalry for military preponderance in South America. On the other hand, if the Kubitschek-Goulart party is duly installed for the next four years, its character and antecedents can hardly fail to sharpen the rivalry between their country and an Argentina governed by anti-Peronistas. It is not beyond the bounds of possibility that such a regime in Brazil might even aid Perón in his effort to stage a comeback in Argentina.

As for its other South American neighbors, Lonardi's

government had correct but hardly cordial relations with Chile and Bolivia and very friendly relations with Uruguay. The government of Chile was headed by a personal friend of Perón's, General Carlos Ibáñez del Campo, and that of Bolivia by a left-wing university professor, Víctor Paz Estenssoro, the backbone of whose support consisted of a kind of organized descamisado element not unlike Peron's C.G.T.— the labor unions of workers in the tin mines.

Little Uruguay was to Lonardi's government what even smaller Paraguay had been to Perón's at the end—its only firm friend among neighboring countries. Lonardi expressed the warmest gratitude to Uruguay for its aid in the long struggle against Perón and showed his appreciation by promptly reopening the once-profitable Argentine tourist trade to Uruguay which Perón had shut off, partly as a political reprisal though also in order to conserve foreign exchange; and as a concession to Uruguayan liberalism, the conservative government at Buenos Aires sent as its ambassador to Montevideo Argentina's best-known Socialist, Alfredo Palacios.

How long this honeymoon between the military dictatorship of Argentina and the civilian, democratic government of Uruguay will last is quite uncertain. Gratitude is a notoriously shifting sand for friendship between nations. Argentina's foreign exchange problem was worse under Lonardi than it ever was under Perón—the *peso* tumbled sharply in the weeks following his overthrow and in October it was devaluated. Moreover, Uruguay, which is the Belgium of South America, a buffer state between its two much bigger neighbors, has never been happy for long over its relations with either Brazil or Argentina. Under Lonardi, an additional strain was placed on the relations between Montevideo and Buenos Aires, for Uruguay is traditionally anticlerical, though rather mildly so, whereas in Argentina

Perón's fall was followed by a reaction in favor of the Catholic Church.

The negotiation of a concordat with the Vatican was proposed by Lonardi on September 23, in his first full-dress speech after he took power. "As regards the Catholic Church," he said, "I will be very happy if Providence grants me the opportunity to settle all differences which have existed through the conclusion of a concordat." The term "concordat" is applied to agreements between a state and the Pope which are designed to adjust "unusual conflicts of authority not amenable to ordinary political or ecclesiastical laws or ordinances," and, as is well known, the Vatican does not enter into them except on terms which it regards as favorable to the Catholic Church.

As a result, although such "unusual conflicts" have occurred in many Latin American countries since the beginning of independence early in the nineteenth century, relatively few concordats have even been entered into by their governments. Still fewer are now in effect and these involve the countries in which the clerical element is strongest; Colombia is the only one of the larger Latin American states that has one. On the other hand, Mexico, where the church-state conflict was particularly long and bitter, does not have one. Since the conflict in Mexico reached its climax in the 1920s the tension has gradually eased, but the anticlerical tradition in that country has been too strong to permit the government to make the concession to clericalism which to most Latin American minds is signified by the negotiation of a concordat. Nor has Argentina herself ever entered into one, despite the facts that under the Constitution of 1853 the government has always supported the Catholic Church and that until Perón's last year in power anticlericalism was never as virulent in that country as in Mexico. As the late nineteenth-century breach of diplomatic relations between Buenos Aires and the Vatican was occasioned by a controversy which was not global but limited to one specific issue, education, so the healing of the breach was not followed by the conclusion of a concordat.

Against this background one might be justified in describing Lonardi's pronouncement of September 23 as proclerical. Unquestionably his proposal, if carried out, would not merely restore the Catholic Church in Argentina to the status it had held before the beginning of Perón's attack on it, but would make its position stronger than it had ever been before. Moreover, note should be taken of the fact that Lonardi proposed to accomplish this by a means which would make it difficult—though obviously not impossible—for future administrations to undo what he had done, for a concordat is in effect a treaty and as such is not subject to alteration without the consent of both parties. For example, in this case a future anticlerical Argentine Congress would not be able to alter it, much less terminate it, without the consent of the Vatican. On this issue, therefore, Lonardi's Provisional Government advocated an arrangement which, to borrow a well-known phrase, was temporary only in the sense that it was not eternal.

Opposition to this measure, which to many Argentines typified "reactionary Catholicism," probably contributed to Lonardi's overthrow in November. Certainly the proposal of a concordat helps to explain why, from the start, certain left-wing leaders, such as Radical Arturo Frondizi and Socialist Américo Ghioldi, qualified their general admonition to the Argentine people to sink all differences in support of Lonardi's "liberating revolution" by the caveat that they reserved the right to disagree later on about specific issues, for Argentine Radicals as well as Socialists have long been committed to an anticlerical position.

4. Aramburu marks time

When General Aramburu took over the Provisional Presidency from General Lonardi on November 13, not the slightest suggestion of any change in foreign policy was contained in any of the three official explanations of the coup. These were Aramburu's radio speech to the nation that day, and two press releases from the presidential office, one issued the same evening and one the following day. Not one of the three even mentioned foreign policy, though all three asserted in general terms the adherence of Aramburu to the aims of the "liberating revolution" as originally stated by Lonardi in September. Indeed, all three stressed the fact that the overturn had been due to differences over personnel, with the clear implication that it had not been due to differences over policy, either domestic or foreign. The most explicit statement to this effect was contained in the third of these official glosses, the press release issued on November 14, which said:

> "The difference which caused General Lonardi to return his prerogatives to the Armed Forces was due to a difference of opinion over the choice of persons who are to execute the acts of the government. This, and this alone, was the reason for the much-discussed discrepancy."

As statements of intention, these glosses were doubtless sincere, but as statements of fact they left a good deal to be desired. It is quite obvious, indeed, that they contain considerable elements of fiction. One is the fiction that Lonardi surrendered his prerogatives voluntarily, whereas the fact is that these were wrenched out of his hands much against his will. Another is the fiction that personnel changes do not involve policy changes even when, as in the present case, the former are made for the avowed purpose of achieving certain "aims" and "purposes" which were in danger of being lost before the personnel changes were made.

Why did the new administration employ these transparent fictions? They may have been designed in part for their domestic effect, since by minimizing the degree of change from Lonardi's to Aramburu's regime, they would maximize the latter's chance of reconciling Lonardi's adherents to the coup and thus of gaining for itself that universal support of the anti-Peronista Argentines which Lonardi had enjoyed in the first flush of victory over Perón. Mainly, however, these fictions seem to have had a foreign policy objective: they were aimed at strengthening the new government's contention that it was merely a continuation of the Lonardi government and thereby preventing the bothersome question of recognition by foreign governments from being raised.

In accordance with this view, the Aramburu government let it be known that it had no intention of requesting recognition by other governments. Its view was accepted by the latter and on November 22 the Foreign Ministry announced with satisfaction that 49 countries had already "reaffirmed" their desire to "maintain" cordial relations with Argentina. Indeed, in the case of the United States Aramburu was visited by the Assistant Secretary of State in charge of Latin American affairs, Henry F. Holland, who arrived in Buenos Aires on November 30. According to a newspaper report, the purpose of his visit was "to find out how much financial aid the provisional government of Argentina hopes to obtain from the United States." [13]

As noted in an earlier section, one of the most important of all the personnel changes made by Aramburu was in the field of foreign relations. This was the replacement of Víctor Amadeo by Luis A. Podestá Costa as Minister of Foreign Affairs. Nevertheless, the new administration's initial silence regarding foreign policy was hardly broken in the ensuing period of a little more than two weeks down to the closing date of the present account, December 1.[14] This may have been either because Podestá Costa was seventy years of age and had had most of his extensive international experience in the legal rather than the political or the economic field; or because the government was too fully occupied with domestic concerns, such as its "de-Peronization" program; or because it was in fact determined to continue the foreign policies of the Lonardi administration, but wished to do so without fanfare. At any rate, no change in those policies had been announced down to our terminal date. It seems unlikely that the project of a concordat with the Vatican will be pursued, but its abandonment had not been proclaimed by that date.

The only important foreign policy statement that came out of the new administration before the end of our period was made by President Aramburu at his first press conference, November 28, at which no questioning was permitted. In the course of his statement the President pledged his government to comply with Argentina's inter-American commitments and cited specifically an agreement adopted at the Bogotá Conference of 1948 to combat both totalitari-

---

[13] *New York Times,* Dec. 1, 1955.
[14] In his second public address on Nov. 23, President Aramburu was as silent about foreign affairs as he had been in his first, on Nov. 13, discussed above in the text.

anism and international Communism. Another item that had foreign policy implications was his statement forecasting the early return of *La Prensa* to its former owners. These implications were suggested by the *New York Times* correspondent's commentary to the effect that, although the decree relating to *La Prensa* was not yet ready for publication, Aramburu had anticipated its issuance in his press conference "so that the Government's action would not be interpreted as a result of talks the President is scheduled to have this week with Henry F. Holland, United States Assistant Secretary of State . . ." [15] In other words, Aramburu felt that he must be on his guard against offending Argentine national pride by seeming to yield to pressure from the United States in favor of *La Prensa*. Under Lonardi the insistence with which this pressure had been applied, by newspapers and other private sources if not by Washington, had aroused much resentment even among anti-Peronista Argentines, who regarded it as unwarranted interference in Argentine affairs and another expression of Yankee imperialism.

This state of mind is one of the basic factors in Argentine-United States relations, to which we now turn.

[15] *New York Times*, Nov. 29, 1955.

5. Problems facing the United States in its Argentine relations

Before we take up the immediate problems facing the United States in its relations with post-Perón Argentina, we must first take note, however briefly, of certain basic factors in these relations which do not change from year to year or even from decade to decade and which are not altered by changes of administration or regime in either country.

Basic factors

The first basic factor is the great distance which separates the two countries. There has been much glib talk in recent years to the effect that space has been annihilated, but for the most part such talk has been a semantic device employed for political purposes. The fact is of course that space will be annihilated only with the universe itself and until that happens space will continue to be an essential condition of human existence. In 1940 Britain was saved from conquest by the mere twenty-mile width of the English Channel. Nearly six thousand miles of water lie between the United States and Argentina; the distance by air is almost as great; and the distance by land would be even greater if it were possible to go that way—which it is not.

Between these two countries there is no question of conquest, but there is the question of intercourse between their peoples through travel and trade, and this is greatly impeded by the great distance that separates them from each other. For the traveler from the United States, a trip to Buenos Aires is twice as long and twice as expensive as a trip to New York or Paris, and trade with Argentina is similarly handicapped. On the other hand, from Argentina a trip to Western Europe is almost as quick and cheap as to the United States, and this space factor, together with the historical developments mentioned in an earlier section,[16] have given Argentina a strong orientation towards Europe.

The second basic factor is the cultural dissimilarity of the two peoples, one of which is preponderantly Latin, the other "Anglo-Saxon." "Culture" is used here in a broad sense to include not only language and literary culture, but also religion, patterns of social and political behavior, and the ideas men live by. The point at which the two peoples might be thought to resemble each other most closely within this broad range is in fact the one at which the profound difference between them is most apparent. This point is the very close resemblance between the constitutions under which the two countries have been governed for the past hundred years; but this very resemblance underlines the contrast between the political behavior of the two peoples— a contrast which has been marked from the beginning but has become glaring in the past quarter century. Even when such differences are primarily expressed in what are called domestic affairs they play an increasingly important part in the relations between the two countries, both of which have shared in the worldwide trend towards stressing the ideological factor in international relations.

The third basic factor lies in the functional similarity be-

[16] See above, pp. 6o, 63.

tween the two peoples. Paradoxically, this similarity has on balance promoted antagonism between them. We have in mind two functions, one political, the other economic. Politically, the Argentines have long played a leading role in South America and one which, making allowances for their country's much smaller size and resources, is comparable to that of the United States. They have aspired to play it even more effectively, for they are the most dynamic of the South American peoples and are often called, not without reason, the Yankees of South America. As a result, they have resented the rise of the United States to leadership in the whole Western Hemisphere and its consequent intrusion into their sphere of influence, and many of them still denounce "Yankee imperialism" with a fervor reminiscent of the days of Big Stick and Dollar Diplomacy. This state of mind lies at the root both of much of the antagonism that has marked the relations between the two countries in the past half century and also of the coolness Argentina has almost always shown, under whatever regime, towards the Pan American System.

The similarity of economic functions consists in the fact that both countries are large-scale producers of agricultural and pastoral commodities for the world market. In this sense it is true, as has so often been said, that their respective economies are competitive, not complementary. As the present writer has pointed out in another place,[17] recent developments suggest that this familiar saying may lose much of its validity, but it has not done so yet. Moreover, the new government at Buenos Aires has announced that it will shift the emphasis in Argentine economic development from industry, where Perón placed it very strongly during most of his regime, back to agriculture, and this decision does not seem likely to mitigate the competitive element

17 Whitaker, *The United States and Argentina*, pp. 196–197.

in the economic relations of Argentina with the United States.

Fourthly and finally, we may apply the term basic to another factor which, while of recent origin, appears to be firmly fixed. This is the difference between the internationalism to which the United States has become committed in the past fifteen years and the "modified isolationism" to which Argentina has always clung and, barring an unexpected policy revolution, will probably continue to cling under the Provisional Government and its successors, whoever they may be, for some time to come. By "modified" we mean an isolationism which is not complete since it does not bar all alliances, but which gives a very strong preference to bilateral over multilateral security arrangements and has accepted the latter only when the alternative was to be left out, to Argentina's manifest and great disadvantage. This kind of isolationism was adhered to by almost every foreign policy maker in Argentina from José de San Martin and Bernardino Rivadavia at the beginning of independence to Perón. What the latter's chief opponents, the Radicals, objected to in his foreign policy was that it was not isolationist enough. In view of this long record, it would be surprising if the new Argentine government or its successor should take a very long step towards the kind of internationalism which the United States is practising and is also preaching to the nations that call themselves its friends.

Specific problems

In some cases the nature of the specific problems involved in the relations between the United States and post-Perón Argentina is not yet entirely clear, for three reasons. First, the Provisional Government has not yet completed the formulation, or at any rate the announcement, of its foreign policy. In the second place, this government is not only provisional but presumably short-lived, and while the foreign policy commitments which it makes in the present crucial period are likely to shape the course of its successors, there can be no certainty that they will do so.

In the third place, there is also some doubt about the policy of the United States. In this case the doubt arises from uncertainty regarding the relative weight which will be accorded in the period just ahead to the three major categories of its objectives, the political, the economic, and the military. Such choices are always necessary, but in this case the choice seems particularly important and it might become difficult and even painful. For example, if a democratic regime is quickly established in Argentina (as has been promised by both Lonardi and Aramburu), and if the United States government decides to place the main emphasis of its policy on strengthening that regime (as it might do for a variety of reasons, including the effect on Latin America at large), it might well be that this would entail some sacrifice of the economic and military objectives of the United States' current policy regarding Argentina. Doubt as to this question of relative emphasis among objectives is increased by two circumstances: first, that the present government of Argentina came to power by overthrowing one which was developing close cooperation with the United States; and second, that this change coincided with the emergence of the "Geneva spirit," which will have one effect on U.S. policy towards Argentina if the spirit prospers and another if it languishes.

Nevertheless, while we cannot define all the problems in terms of the policies of the two governments, since these are not yet entirely clear, we can with reasonable assurance identify the subjects of chief importance in their relations and, in most cases, indicate what the problems are likely to be. This will be done below in summary form, mainly from

the point of view of the United States and the three main
categories of its objectives just mentioned, namely, economic,
military, and political.

ECONOMIC. Here the three chief subjects, which are obviously interlocking, are trade between the two countries,
U.S. investments in Argentina, and U.S. economic aid to
Argentina. Within the limits set by the basic factors described above, the nature of the problems in these three cases
will depend—largely in the first two, to a considerable degree
in the third—on the extent to which the new Argentine government puts into practice the ideas which its economic adviser, Raúl Prebisch, has already developed theoretically in
ECLA.[18] If these prevail, the United States may face a situation in which its trade and investments will be cramped
by government controls which, though more rational and
better administered than Perón's, may be even more rigorous,
and in which Argentina's demand for government-to-government aid will outweigh its encouragement to private investment. To date, the trend of the new government's policy
has been away from regimentation towards free enterprise,
but it is still too early to say what the final outcome will be.

U.S. economic aid might prove to be the key to this situation. Hitherto Argentina has received little aid of this kind.
This was not only, or even mainly, because until 1953 the
relations between the United States and Perón's Argentina
varied only from cold to cool. It was rather because, first,
as a country of "intermediate" economic development, Argentina fell between two stools of U.S. foreign aid policy in
the sense that it has been the policy of the United States to
aid either industrial countries (as under the Marshall Plan)
or underdeveloped countries (as more recently in Asia), and
Argentina is neither. It was also because U.S. economic aid
has been concentrated in those areas which are critical in the

[18] See above, pp. 109–110.

cold war, and Latin America, including Argentina, has not been deemed a critical area. For reasons that cannot be developed here—they relate to the underlying assumptions of the economic aid program, its record to date, and the "Geneva spirit"—a strong argument might be made for re-thinking this program. If that were done, a strong argument could also be made for intensifying it in the case of Argentina because of the economic wreckage left by the Perón regime and because of the benefits, both economic and political, that might accrue to the United States, not to mention humanitarian considerations.

Admittedly, however, this problem is as difficult as it is important. At the present writing, the specific form in which U.S. aid to Argentina is being most earnestly discussed is that of a general-purpose loan. From Washington's point of view, both the pros and the cons of this question are impressive. On the one hand, it would greatly strengthen the anti-Peronista regime in Argentina by enabling it, among other things, to solve its vitally important oil problem by the only means which seems politically feasible at present, namely, by rehabilitating and expanding its own governmental agency, Y.P.F. On the other hand, the very fact that a large part of the loan would be used to finance Y.P.F. raises two serious objections: first, it would conflict with the general policy of not aiding foreign governmental agencies in fields deemed appropriate to private enterprise; and second, it might open the door to demands for U.S. aid to similar government petroleum agencies in Brazil (Petrobras) and Mexico (Pemex).[19]

Among the economic problems one may also note the rising protest in Argentina, as well as in other food-exporting countries, against what they regard as the unfair com-

[19] This problem is discussed in *Hanson's Latin American Letter,* No. 554, Washington, Oct. 29, 1955.

petition of the United States government's surplus food stocks in the world market. Finally, if the recovery of the Argentine beef industry takes place as planned, it may lead to the revival of a once bitter controversy of which relatively little has been heard in recent years—the controversy over the United States' exclusion of all fresh beef from Argentina because of the existence of the hoof-and-mouth disease in certain parts of that country.

MILITARY. Problems in the military field are currently brought to a focus by the question of a bilateral military pact with the United States, which Argentine Foreign Minister Amadeo spoke of on October 11, 1955, as under study by his government. We have already noted that under Perón important opposition elements in Argentina had offered strong resistance to security arrangements of this kind. Now that the opposition is in power, the first question is whether it will consent to the projected bilateral pact, but there is also a second question which the changed situation in Argentina and the rest of the world emphasizes. This is whether, from the point of view of the United States and in view of Argentina's relatively low military potential, such a pact would be worth the cost. It would offend many of the most democratic elements in Argentina, as the negotiation of similar pacts has already done in other Latin American countries. One of the most cogent objections to it is that it is likely to strengthen the already too powerful military elements in those countries. This objection loses none of its force in Argentina, for if its armed forces liberated the country from Perón's tyranny, it was also they who helped to bring him to power and sustain him for ten years, and before that they had set up military dictatorships in 1930 and 1943. At any rate, this is a problem that requires a nice balance between the military objective and the other objectives of American foreign policy.

POLITICAL. The political problems of the United States with reference to Argentina are deeply enmeshed with its economic and military problems, as even the brief foregoing discussion of the latter has suggested. There is, however, one fundamentally important question which can be considered as a purely political one and which has implications that extend to all the other Latin American countries, if not still further. This is the question whether the United States should, in the interest of freedom, exert itself to strengthen the government of General Aramburu and the democratic government which he promises will quickly grow out of his dictatorship. Obviously, the question is a part of the whole thorny problem of intervention and nonintervention, which we can only sketch lightly here.

As is well known, this problem is old and worldwide, but for the United States it has been important only since about 1900 and, because of the concurrent growth of Pan Americanism, its importance has been confined mainly—at first exclusively—to Latin America. From 1904 until the 1920s the United States practiced intervention, ostensibly for three major purposes: to forestall European intervention (thereby, among other things, protecting the Panama Canal), to correct conditions of "chronic wrongdoing and impotence" in certain countries, and to facilitate the United States' civilizing mission. Unimpressed by this high motivation, Latin Americans reacted against intervention, slowly at first, but violently in the end, for it seemed to them simply an instrument of Yankee imperialism. Argentina, it should be noted, led the attack.

Accordingly, in the interest of Pan American harmony, the United States gradually abandoned both the theory and the practice of intervention. The climax came in 1936 when the United States carried its Good Neighbor Policy to the point of signing a permanent inter-American treaty which placed an absolute ban on intervention; the treaty was duly ratified by the Senate in 1937 and is still in effect. Moreover, the United States has also signed and ratified the Bogotá Charter of the Organization of American States (1948), in which the ban is repeated. This might have seemed to close the door to further discussion of intervention as a matter of U.S. foreign policy, since this country is now solemnly and doubly committed to absolute nonintervention.

The matter is not so simple as that, however, and in the past dozen years a number of avenues have been found for reopening the question. In the first place, it has been argued that the 1936 ban applies only to unilateral intervention, by a single country, so that multilateral intervention is still permissible. In the second place, the Bogotá Charter actually does make an exception to the ban in favor of multilateral security measures taken under the Rio Treaty of 1947. In the third place, it has been argued that further exceptions to the ban are required for the enforcement of the guarantees of human rights contained in the charters of the United Nations and the OAS. In the fourth place, in the absence of a full and authoritative definition of intervention, strict constructionists argue that the ban applies only to forcible intervention, or specifically to the use of armed force. Acceptance of that view would not only permit positive measures in support of approved governments, but would also, in cases of disagreement, leave strong nations free to employ very potent means of coercing weaker ones, without violating the ban on intervention. Yet, if we are to be realistic, it must be admitted that no definition of the term is ever likely to be found which will greatly reduce the power of strong nations over weaker ones.

This consequence of the inequality of power has furnished the ground for still another argument against nonintervention in which the premise is more articulate than the conclusion. The premise was well stated in a *New York Times* editorial of October 12, 1955, which said: ". . . It can never be forgotten that the United States is so powerful economically and politically that whatever we do or do not do greatly affects the individual Latin-American countries, and in that sense is a form of intervention, whether we intend it or not." The conclusion would seem to be that since the United States cannot help intervening in Latin America, it should intervene deliberately, intelligently, and of course on the right side. This conclusion is seldom publicly stated in so many words. Indeed, many who start from the premise that points to it stop at some undefined point short of it. Thus, in the *Times* editorial just quoted, nonintervention was described as "a precious and necessary principle of hemispheric affairs." But privately the conclusion has been explicitly stated with increasing frequency in the past fifteen years. It will be interesting to see whether, and if so how, it is applied to the important test case presented by the current situation in Argentina—a case which, we repeat, is potentially of great significance for the whole Latin American policy of the United States.

In conclusion, without venturing to pass judgment on the complex question of intervention, which requires far more thorough discussion than has been possible in these pages, the present writer wishes to point out that the events of the past dozen years in Argentina illustrate a consideration which should never be overlooked. This is that if, as many assure us, nonintervention is no longer a feasible policy for the United States, on the other hand history shows that, whether the term intervention is used in the broad or the narrow sense, interventions by the United States in Latin America have almost never been successful and have often produced results opposite to those intended. This has happened twice in Argentina since 1943. In the first three years the United

States exerted heavy pressure (though without using armed force) to prevent the rise of Perón to power, and the present writer, who has discussed this question with many Argentines of all shades of political opinion, has not found one who did not believe that this interference of the United States in the domestic affairs of Argentina was self-defeating and helped Perón in his rise to power. A decade later the United States had reversed its attitude and was now giving positive support to Perón, and this support was unquestionably a factor, and possibly a major factor, in bringing about his downfall.

Consequently, if the United States wishes to strengthen the present regime in Buenos Aires, it could do worse than stir up a sharp diplomatic controversy with the authorities there. Whatever aid it is willing to provide could then be offered as the price of peace, thus giving the new regime one of those victories over the Colossus of the North which, in Perón's palmy days, did so much to win the plaudits of his fellow countrymen and strengthen his hold on power. This would cost no more than we were, by hypothesis, already prepared to pay and the "defeat," which would do no harm to so strong a nation as the United States, would make possible the realization of the assumed objective of its policy. At any rate, the clamant nationalism of smaller countries such as Argentina poses problems for the United States to which, if experience is any guide, the new interventionism does not provide the answer.

EPILOGUE

Epilogue on a kaleidoscope

Juan Perón's Argentine tyranny lasted only a decade, whereas Francisco Franco has ruled Spain ever since early 1939
and shows no signs yet of losing his grip. Perhaps this means
that freedom is a hardier plant in Argentina than in Spain,
in America than in Europe. Or it may mean that Perón's
enemies were not deterred from taking up arms against him
by memories of a frightful civil war such as those that make
countless Spaniards acquiesce in the continuance of Franco's
rule rather than risk a repetition of the horror.

Or again it may only mean that Argentina is more unstable
than Spain. Certainly, as we look back over the history of
Argentina since the 1920s we cannot fail to be struck by the
high degree of instability that has characterized it. Perón's
ten-year domination is only an apparent exception, for under-
neath the surface uniformity of his rule there was a constant
shifting of posture and direction, which was accentuated
after Eva Perón's death in 1952 and which reached its peak
in his last year at the helm.

Now that the specious stability of the Perón era is gone,
the kaleidoscopic character of Argentine public life stands
starkly revealed again. The Lonardi regime which succeeded
Perón's was in turn ousted within eight weeks. To be sure,
the new Aramburu regime claimed that it was a continuation

of its predecessor, with a somewhat different personnel, so that the change was one not of government but only of administration, and its view was accepted by foreign governments, for whom it was designed. But this legal fiction need not be taken seriously outside official circles, and even if it were accepted at face value it could not alter the fact that the Lonardi administration was forced out by a military coup after less than two months in power—a fact which indicates a high degree of instability in the current Argentine political situation.

The prospects for an early improvement in this regard are not bright. Aramburu has indeed started out with ostensibly unanimous support both from the armed forces and from all the political parties and groups except the Communists and the Peronistas. This is no guarantee of stability, however, for Lonardi's start was even more auspicious since, in addition to all these elements, he had the support of the "reactionaries" subsequently ousted by Aramburu. Also, it is no guarantee because the armed forces are divided by interservice rivalries and the political parties are divided not only by their differences with one another but also by their own internal rifts, which have split one of the oldest political parties, the Radicals, and the newest of the political groups, the Christian Democrats, as well as the Socialists and the Communists. The trend towards political fragmentation in present-day Argentina is strong, and it may be increased rather than diminished by the recent suppression of the men's and women's Peronista parties.

The differences among political parties and between civilians and the military in Argentina are not mere matters of opinion over which there is agreement to disagree and to settle the question at the polls. They have been fought over before and they may be fought over again, for they are rooted in the social and economic and cultural soil of Argentina. Of the many explosive factors in the current Argentine situation, two stand out at the present writing. One is the disastrous financial and economic condition of the country, which can hardly fail to aggravate the already serious social and political tensions. The other is the commitment of the majority Radical group to a platform calling for a total and revolutionary transformation of the economic and social life of Argentina, with a list of specifications which is sure to arouse widespread and bitter opposition.

The prospect of stability is perhaps better under the present Provisional Government than under its putative democratic successor, for the former is a military dictatorship and the armed forces, despite their interservice and other rivalries, are probably more homogeneous than the political parties. Even now, however, a potential element of serious discord has been introduced by an arrangement which may have been quite well-intentioned, namely, the sharing of the military dictatorship's responsibility, but not its power, with the civilian National Consultative Council. The pot will certainly begin to boil when the government is handed back to the civilians, as promised, for the majority Radicals, the highly controversial character of whose program has just been noted, are already the country's largest party and are now making a strong bid for the big ex-Peronista vote. And if the civilian government does not function as the armed forces think it should, they may be expected to take over again in the fulfillment of their self-appointed mission to save Argentina by serving as the ultimate arbiter of the nation's political disputes.

If any Latin American nation could overcome such a sea of troubles, it should be the Argentines, for they are in many ways the most advanced and most talented of the twenty members of the Latin American family. If they fail to do so in the near future, it will be because, despite their many fine qualities and their splendid traditions of civic life, they are now a deeply and multiply divided nation.

Political stability and its concomitant, public order, are far from being the chief virtues of a nation, just as the lack of them is by no means the worst vice. Yet it is only when a people are not continually harassed by political instability and public disorder that they can duly cultivate the things in life that make it worth while. This hard lesson the Argentines have learned to their cost in the past quarter century. Two lessons from this experience should be noted by policy makers in the United States. One is that in dealing with so unstable a country as Argentina, policy should not be based upon the type of government in that country; the other, that one of the few constants in the shifting sands of Argentine opinion is a pronounced anti-imperialism which is tinged with Yankeephobia and yet is not wholly unlike the animus against Wall Street that once inspired agrarian revolts in the United States itself.

APPENDICES

Appendix 1

CHRONOLOGY

1943

June 4. A group of Argentine Army officers seizes the government. Col. Juan Perón, a member of the group, begins his rise to power.

1945

October 9. Perón's fellow Army officers force him to resign all his government posts (Vice President, Minister of War, and Secretary of Labor and Social Welfare).

October 17. Perón is brought back in triumph by the descamisados and regains Army support, but confirms his resignations to become a candidate for the presidency.

October 21. Perón marries Eva Duarte.

1946

June 4. Perón is inaugurated President for six years.

1949

March 16. Perón proclaims a "reformed" Constitution which permits his re-election.

1951

September 28. Part of the Army revolts. The revolt is suppressed the same day.

1952

June 4. Perón is inaugurated for a second term.
July 26. Eva Duarte de Perón dies of cancer.

1954

November. Perón begins to attack the Roman Catholic Church.

1955

June 16. Perón's excommunication is announced. Air elements of the Navy and Air Force revolt but are suppressed by the Army.

July 5. Perón makes a conciliatory speech calling for a cessation of political strife. On July 15 he follows this up by resigning as head of the Peronista Party and announcing the end of his twelve-year revolution.

July 28. Arturo Frondizi, Radical leader, replies in a radio speech that there can be no peace without freedom. Strife continues.

August 31. Perón offers his resignation as President but withdraws it and makes an incendiary speech when the General Confederation of Labor (C.G.T.) stages "another October 17 [1945]."

September 16. A "liberating revolution" is proclaimed at Córdoba by General Eduardo Lonardi and is supported by parts of all branches of the armed forces.

September 19. Perón again offers his resignation, which is accepted. He takes refuge on a Paraguayan gunboat at Buenos Aires.

September 23. General Lonardi, as Provisional President, transfers the military government of Argentina from Córdoba to Buenos Aires and promises speedy restoration of constitutional, democratic government.

November 13. The armed forces oust President Lonardi on the ground that he has reactionary advisers. General Pedro Eugenio Aramburu replaces him as Provisional President and promises to restore the liberating revolution to its original path.

November 30. President Aramburu decrees the abolition of the
Peronista Party (already decided by Lonardi) and the return
of the newspaper *La Prensa* from the C.G.T. to its former
owners. U.S. Assistant Secretary of State Henry F. Holland
arrives for discussions with him.

Appendix 2

DOCUMENTS

The following documents, which consist mainly of extracts from speeches by leading Argentines, illustrate points made in the text about the Argentine upheaval from early June to the end of November 1955. No. 1 gives Perón's version of the bitter Church-State controversy on the eve of the abortive revolt of June 16. No. 2 comes from Radical leader Arturo Frondizi's challenging reply to Perón's call for pacification on July 5. Nos. 3, 4, and 5 are respectively Perón's first offer to resign and the ritual negative replies of the C.G.T. and the men's Peronista Party, the latter calling for "another October 17." No. 6 is General Eduardo Lonardi's pronunciamento at the beginning of the successful revolt against Perón. In No. 7 Lonardi, now Provisional President, reveals the gravity of the economic situation. Nos. 8 and 9 explain why Lonardi was ousted in favor of General Pedro Eugenio Aramburu. No. 10 is Aramburu's first comprehensive public statement of his policies; it was made only a week before the end of the period covered in this book.

The text of the following documents was taken from English translations of Argentine radio broadcasts. In each case the code letters of the station and the day and hour of the broadcast are given. Omissions are indicated in the usual way: . . . Because of considerations of space the omissions have been extensive at several points, since these documents are designed only to provide the reader with a sampling and it seemed desirable to make the sampling as large as possible. While it is believed that the translations convey the sense of the original, circumstances make it impossible to guarantee their complete accuracy.

1. *Perón on the Church-State Controversy*

[Speech by President Perón broadcast from the Presidential residence, LRA Buenos Aires (Official), Argentine Home Service, June 13, 1955, 11:30 p.m.]

Once again our unrelenting struggle for the liberation of the Argentine people has come face to face with the forces of reaction and their violent methods . . . In August 1943, I told the Argentine people that we had finished the fight against our enemies both inside and outside the nation. At that time, I invited all Argentines to work together in peace. The people saw the need for this. For some time the oligarchy was apparently willing to accept this atmosphere of peace, but the part of the oligarchy which never completely abandoned the struggle was the clerical oligarchy. For 12 years the Government tried by every means possible to establish complete harmony by granting ecclesiastical guarantees. I believed that this was possible. I also felt that the Argentine people wanted the Government to create better conditions for the spiritual action of a religious nature, as the specific work of the Church should be . . .

Unfortunately, a certain segment of the clergy, whose materialism and pride has now marked practically all the ecclesiastical hierarchies, could not be persuaded that we were doing the right thing . . . Our future action shall be against those that make [improper] use of the people, against the bad hierarchs of the Church and against their organizations, which try to promote through the Cathedral and the temples the interests of the oligarchy which the people rejected in October 1945 . . .

How can we permit officials of the State—as members of the ecclesiastical hierarchy are—to be the promoters of disorders and outrageous depredations against the properties and the dignity of the Nation, expressly and with premeditation disobeying judicious decisions of the authorities which were aimed at preventing them? . . . Undoubtedly, either the clergy has lost all control, or if not, this is a case of subversive acts, which the Government, in defense of order, is obligated to prevent by any means. This warning is directed to those who are naively serving unacknowledged interests . . . The people are already getting tired of their impertinences of all kinds, and some day they may provoke reactions the consequences of which it is difficult to foresee. One cannot offend with impunity the people, their institutions, and their symbols without expecting an immediate penalty.

The fact that this has not already occurred on different occasions is due to my personal efforts to prevent it. I am not sure, however, that these admirable and patient Argentine people—who in this case also show themselves to be our best possessions—may not get tired one day and decide to take justice into their own hands.

In this connection, I once again address the people, recommending that they be calm, although to remain so they may have to resort to all their will power. What has happened is a case for the police, and it will be settled by the police and the courts, without prejudice to the administrative measures which the Government will adopt to safeguard its authority and its prestige . . .

As a matter of general conduct, it is necessary to recall the watchword of the hours of vigilance and observation: "From work to home and from home to work" . . . For every man that our enemies can put up against us, we can put up 10 and 10 times as many men as theirs. Therefore, I recommend calm and tranquillity.

We are serious minded persons and we are also responsible persons. We should not stage spectacles such as those which they put on. Our organizations, disciplined and organic, cannot [afford to] lose their prestige in unimportant and unproductive bickerings. Good night.

2. *Frondizi's Reply to Perón's Pacification Offer*

[Speech by Arturo Frondizi, leader of the Radical Party, LRY Buenos Aires, in Spanish to Argentina, July 28, 1955, 12:30 a.m.]

In my capacity as president of the National Committee of the Unión Cívica Radical [Radical Party], I wish to address myself to the country to express the attitude of Radicalism in this difficult hour for the Nation.

The President of the Republic has announced his plan for bringing peace to the country, and he requested the opinion of the political parties . . . We must remember that the national convention of the Unión Cívica Radical in its session of Dec. 8, 1952, issued a resolution in which it categorically asserted the need for harmonious living among all Argentines. On that occasion, we made a solemn appeal to the sense of national responsibility in order that, with a patriotic vision, harmonious relationships and unification could be restored among the Argentines. These are based on a return to loyal obedience to the Constitution and the effective implementation of the guarantees which complement human dignity.

Our ideals were based on that then, and our ideals are based on that now. Before going into these ends—the indispensable requirements for pacification—we must enumerate four warnings:

(1) Since its inception into Argentine civic life, the Radical Party has advocated from a distance and has carried out while in the administration thorough fulfillment and implementation of the national Constitution. Therefore, the Radical Party believes that pacification should come about through a strict adherence to the Constitution, and accordingly does not accept, under any excuse, any solution which might in any way restrict or infringe upon the republican, representative, and federal form of government.

(2) I will not go into the causes of the national drama. Radicalism is not motivated by rancor, hatred, or the desire to even the score. It does not come to offend nor to lay the blame on anyone, but to expose the large ideas behind which Argentina's

unification can be made possible. In addition, this struggle has never been directed against personalities or groups of persons, but against political and social systems, both past and current, which, if they subsisted, would deny loftiness and nobleness to the future.

(3) Pacification cannot and must not be a new form of submission. We want peace, but not at the cost of our freedom or through the abandonment of our democratic ideals. We wish to affirm here and now that before relinquishing a single one of those rights, we prefer to be persecuted because of our loyalty to the cause of the people and not enjoy the conspiratorial calmness which could be attained by being treasonable to the people.

(4) The Unión Cívica Radical wishes to point out and underscore concrete facts. Pacification can come about only by fulfilling a group of objective conditions that will restore morality and democracy to the country—morality and democracy which cannot be substituted by verbal promises.

With these qualifications, I can now go into the concrete measures indispensable to bringing about an atmosphere of peace that will allow for elevated and constructive discussion of the large national issues, of the [problems], and of the Government programs . . .

The Argentine revolution which started in 1810 has not ended, although it has suffered stoppages, and has been led astray. This process coincides with the world revolution and transformation now in full progress, in which the social aspects play an important role. The statement made by the President of the Republic to the effect that popular political parties will respect and perfect social conquests is completely correct insofar as the Radical Party is concerned.

No step back in this respect is possible, although many steps will be taken forward. To return to a regime of freedom does not presuppose a return to old conservative criteria. Freedom is not a mere formal expression. Freedom, to be complete and effective, must reach the depth of social relations and eliminate from them all the causes of insecurity, greed, and moral neglect.

When the Unión Cívica Radical speaks of perfecting the conquests achieved by the workers over many years of struggle, it means three things: (1) The conquests will apply to all sectors of the population and will grant ever-greater participation in national life; (2) they will cover all aspects of social and individual life, so that those who work may be really protected throughout all the phases of their lives; (3) these conquests will have a new basis, depending not on the will of one man or a party, but on the law and the existence of powerful union organizations which should be founded on freedom of unionization, the right to strike, and political independence . . .

In the field of international policy, the country cannot continue on a vacillating road, which places it alternately at the mercy of one or another imperialist. We cannot continue to speculate on the possibility of a world war which would postpone the solution of serious national problems. The Argentine nation should follow an independent international policy, specifically and positively its own, based on an understanding of the political sovereignty of the country, as well as on the economic and social sovereignty of the people.

It is necessary to maintain these three types of sovereignty, and on them to build an international policy which would strengthen the brotherhood of our American countries and would place Argentina in the position of a country in the service of democracy and brotherhood of the nations of the world, and of mankind in general . . .

Although the Radical Party does not have material power, it is the owner of immense moral strength because of deep loyalty to its spiritual meaning and to its history and a heart and mind devoted to the fatherland and the people. The Radical Party is not going to waste its moral strength. Therefore, in this hour of anxious expectation, we join the people of Argentina who always want to live in the full possession of their democratic rights, free from hatred and fear, and liberated from the burden of cultural, economic, and social privileges.

May the Government know how to carry out its duty to Argentina, which the present situation demands. The Unión Cívica Radical knows how to fulfill its duty.

3. *Perón's First Resignation Offer*

[President Perón's statement to the General Confederatian of Labor and the two Peronista parties, LRA Buenos Aires (Official), in Spanish to Argentina, Aug. 31, 1955, 1:30 p.m.]

Some declarations by our adversaries and political enemies, to the effect that they make their attitude conditional on my retirement from the Government, have reached me.

I have always been a man with an open mind, and I believe that, even though I am in office through the will of the overwhelming majority of the Argentine people, the dignity of the post and my manly honor require me to offer my resignation.

It is undeniable that by this action I offer our Movement a solution, with the thought that I can be used for the good of the Nation and to strengthen the Movement against the enemies of the people. For this Movement enjoys popular support without precedent in the Nation's political history. At the same time, the Movement will be able to contemplate the final stage of its organizational work as a political institution of the Argentine people . . .

It is the hour for Argentines to come to an understanding and to consolidate all that we have offered them with our struggle, our labor, and our sacrifice. The time has passed for reforms and strife. Now work and consolidation must be achieved.

In the same manner in which I formerly offered my life to correct injustice, and to remedy the social and economic evils afflicting the Nation, I believe the moment has come to offer my resignation if it would be a guarantee of pacification . . .

To achieve definitive pacification, other men whose strength has not been spent in the effort can advantageously replace us . . . We, as profound reformers, find difficulty in being good pacifiers and stabilizers. This is the task of other men who can be satisfied with perfecting the things created by us, and not of those who have a permanent creative spirit . . .

I have heard whispers that my disappearance will bring on a grave problem. I do not believe that will be the case, and even if it were, I would do better to disappear calmly, averting all disorder, in accord with the law which all have the obligation to respect.

Some thoughtless and speculative politicians, with the aim of causing agitation, speak of civil war. There will be no civil war here. There will be peace or dictatorship.

I do not have the character to be a dictator, so that if such an eventuality should occur, another, or others will have to replace me . . . The changing of one man, regardless of his importance, should not give rise to the disruption of the lives of millions of men. Because of this I humbly ask the millions of Argentines who have trusted me to free me from all commitments and accept my departure from the Government, so that I can take my place as a simple Peronista in our Movement . . .

Man has always been an obstacle to the establishment of institutions. The gregarious spirit which gives birth to a *caudillo* is in itself an enemy of organization. But neither the man nor the caudillo can conquer time. Doctrine and organization do. Because of this the wise and prudent road is to replace the man with the doctrine and the institution . . .

I was elected by the people's sovereign will in the purest election ever held in Argentina's political history. It is to this sovereign will which I now appeal, demanding my own freedom of action.

I wanted the Peronista Party, the members of its men's and women's branches, and the Secretariat of the General Confederation of Labor, to be the recipients of this communication. It is from them that I derive the corresponding authority to act in the manner of which I have spoken.

4. *C. G. T. Rejects Perón's Offer*

[LRA Buenos Aires (Official), in Spanish to Argentina, Aug. 31, 1955, 3:45 p.m.]

The General Labor Confederation, C.G.T., makes the following announcement:

The general strike ordered by the central headquarters is in full effect throughout the Nation. The workers have suspended their activities without exception.

The Argentine labor movement expresses its fervent support for the Chief Magistrate, Gen. Perón, and its irrevocable decision that he should continue to guide the destinies of the Republic.

5. *Peronista Party Calls for "Another October 17"*

[Summary of rebroadcast of speech by Alejandro H. Leloir, President of the men's Peronista Party Superior Council, LRY Buenos Aires, in Spanish to Argentina, Aug. 31, 1955, 6:25 p.m.]

As president of the Peronista Party Superior Council I have received from President Perón a document in which he offers to the country his resignation from the popular mandate if this can, to use his own words, guarantee pacification . . .

My General, you have to remain. To reaffirm this idea I give this single reminder to you, who have carried out history with loftiness and moreover have been doing so every day for 10 years: San Martín once returned to the country desirous of putting the sword which liberated America at the service of Argentine freedom. He could not disembark, and he had to die in exile, sad because he saw his people divided, confused, and broken into fragments by the ambition and pettiness of small politicians.

This is not now the case. Go shortly to the plaza of victory. At the Plaza de Mayo you will find the people united and strongly organized.

To the Argentine citizenry, only one order: To the Plaza de Mayo and to all the plazas of the Republic for another October 17. (Applause and shouts of Perón, and Perón, yes; another, no.)

6. *Lonardi Proclaims "Liberating Revolution"*

[Proclamation of Freedom Speech by Gen. Eduardo Lonardi, September 16. Rebroadcast, LRA Buenos Aires (Official), Argentine Home Service, September 22, 1955, 4 p.m.]

To the Argentine people and to the soldiers of the fatherland:

In my capacity as leader of the liberating revolution, I address the people and especially my comrades of all branches of the Armed Forces, to request their cooperation in our movement.

The Navy, the Air Force, and the Army of the fatherland are leaving their bases and garrisons once more to intervene in the civic life of the Nation. We do so impelled by the imperative love for freedom and honor of a subjugated people who want to live in accordance with traditions and who do not resign themselves to following indefinitely the whims of a dictator who abuses the powers of government in order to humiliate his fellow citizens. Under the pretext of strengthening the principles of a social justice which no one disputes because at the present time it is the common aspiration of all Argentines, he has annihilated the rights and guarantees of the Constitution and suppressed the juridical order by his domineering and despotic will.

This ignoble oppression has only served for the rapid increase of corruption and for the destruction of culture and economy, of which [eloquent?] examples are the burning of the temples and of the [national?] archives of the fatherland, the political dependence of the judiciary, the reduction of the universities to a dishonest bureaucracy, and the tragic [one word unintelligible] which endangers the future of the Republic through the surrender of its sources of wealth.

If this fantastic picture promotes the disquietude of the Argentines, the dictator, after [signing?] his resignation, offers them the prospect of civil war and of brothers killing each other, looking forward to the possibility of putting to death five of his unarmed oppositionists for each one of his followers and torturers. It is not strange that he lends himself to participation in profaning the flag in order to charge his enemies with the sacrilege. Before our fellow citizens and posterity, we accuse him of unspeakable villainy, fully proved by the investigations carried out by the Supreme War and Marine Council.

The concern for honor and freedom which had been violated by tyranny found fertile ground in the hearts of the young officers who, with a rare unanimity, disdained gratuities and corruption, putting their immaculate swords at the service of civic ideals.

The many officers who throughout the territory of Argentina ratify this proclamation with their names and with their blood applaud this youthful initiative which revindicates for all time the prestige of the National Army and places all of them on the level of their immortal forerunners; namely, those who decorated the churches with the trophies taken from the enemy, who gave shining glory to our insignia in the battles which created the fatherland, and who gave never equalled examples of unselfishness and sacrifice.

The members of the Armed Forces must not entertain any scruple because of the alleged legality of the mandate which the dictator exhibits. No democracy is legitimate in which the essential prerequisites, freedom and guarantees of personal rights, do not exist, in which the poll lists are fraudulent, or where in public assemblies the expression of the will of the people is falsified. On the other hand, [democracy?] can call upon the article of the Constitution currently in effect which directs the Argentine people to take up arms in defense of the Constitution and of the laws, and on the article which labels as "infamous traitors to the fatherland" those who grant extraordinary powers which are [one word unintelligible] in their application.

Our brother workers may know that we pledge our honor as soldiers when we promise solemnly that we shall never consent to the [abridgement] of their rights. The legitimate conquests which protect them will not only be maintained but expanded through a spirit of Christian solidarity and the freedom to [improve?] legislation because order and administrative honesty will benefit everyone.

The revolution is not carried out for the benefit of parties, classes, or trends, but to reestablish the power of the law. Prostrated at the feet of the Virgin our leader, and invoking the protection of God, source of all reason and justice, we have issued this [proclamation] for all those who make up the Armed Forces of the Nation, officers, noncommissioned officers, and soldiers, so that they will place themselves together with us in the [battle line?] which the Great Captain's example points out to us.

We say this simply, after long and careful deliberation: The sword that we have unsheathed to defend the symbols of the fatherland we will keep with honor only. We are not interested in life without honor, and to reach our objective we pledge the future of our children and the dignity of our families.

(Signed) Eduardo Lonardi, Division General, Chief of the Liberating Revolution.

7. *Lonardi on the Disastrous Economic Situation*

[Speech by Provisional President Eduardo Lonardi, LRA Buenos Aires (Official), Argentine Home Service, Oct. 26, 1955, 11:30 p.m.]

To all the Argentine people: I spoke to the people of the Republic during the memorable revolution to invite them to fulfill their constitutional mandate and rise in arms to defend liberty. Later, in Buenos Aires, I again spoke to sketch the broad lines of my Government program. Today, it behooves me to report to the Nation on the gravest problem before us, namely, the economic situation.

The system of hiding truth has terminated forever. The Nation desires to know the truth, regardless of how dire and painful it may be.

Ten years of irresponsibility and corruption have carried us to a most disastrous situation in the economic field. The Nation has tried to accomplish what no one could fulfill, and impelled by a tremendous [insatiability?] it has tried to consume more than it has produced. In this way, it spent its monetary reserves. It has lived on its capital and caused an overwhelming internal deficit which carried the public debt to an unprecedented figure, while the foreign indebtedness has brought about the accumulation of a mass of disquieting obligations to foreign countries.

I have not come to make promises, or to promise generalities. I address the Nation not to give, but to ask something of it, and to outline the urgent steps needed at this pressing moment. I have come to ask for the people's energies, their [support?], and sacrifice . . .

But this foreign debt is not our most serious trouble. If our Nation's exports were normal, as in other times, we could easily pay off this foreign debt. However, we are no longer the great exporting Nation we once were. On a pro-rata basis, our exports per capita during the last five-year period were only half those of the five prewar years.

This is the main reason for our unfavorable foreign indebtedness. We lack the necessary foreign exchange to import the raw materials and equipment indispensable to the normal development of our economic activities. However, we will adopt urgent measures to remedy this.

To the export crisis we must add the results of the petroleum policy, and the equally disastrous agriculture and livestock policy.

There has been lack of foresight in providing the increasingly rising consumer needs, while petroleum imports, which formerly constituted only a tenth part of the total national imports, today constitute a fifth part. This drastically curtails the importation of essential needs. To solve this situation, the deposed Government entered into unacceptable arrangements which the entire Nation repudiated, and which filled public opinion with consternation. It is not true that we Argentines lack the ability to produce petroleum through our own efforts. In a relatively short time we will be able to double current production, and later, through persistent efforts, we will cover our own needs.

Despite this, this Government believes it is advantageous to utilize foreign public and private capital and foreign technical knowledge to promote a vigorous petroleum development program.

We believe in the system of free enterprise, which has contributed so much to the development of western civilization, because it is not incompatible with the State's sane economic policy. An increase in petroleum production will permit us to effect great savings of foreign exchange, making it possible to import other foreign capital goods.

But this is not enough. The Nation needs more foreign exchange and to obtain it we must face the pressing task of stepping up agricultural and livestock production, and must greatly expand our exports.

The gravest error of the deposed Government was to promote industrialization while suppressing the loyal farm producer and his productive labor and disillusioning the rural workers. This brought on a drastic drop in production, and consequently the export crisis.

The Government will exert its fullest energies to restore production from our soil. It will grant planting quotas to the producers, and supply the resources needed to bring our agricultural production up to the most advanced technical level, so as to increase the rate of production rapidly and so that we can regain the desired position regarding exports.

Unfortunately, all this requires time, and there is a vital need for capital goods, especially in the production of electric power, and in the field of transportation . . .

In Argentina obsolete economic and social systems doubtless existed, which had to be overcome by imposing a clear-cut social policy. However, "justicialism" has consisted of a system which extended the obsolete systems to newly rich groups, which are the living symbols of the presumptive "third position" between capitalism and Communism. Its ideology has lacked sincerity and conviction, and the contradictions of the regime stem from this fact. "Justicialism" starts by detesting foreign capital, and ends by negotiating the vast petroleum concessions. It proclaims the Nation's economic independence, and leaves it in an extremely vulnerable financial position with insufficient funds to pay for the essential imports . . .

Behind the tinfoil and the frills we find a kind of sinister game being played by destructive children, who simulate correctness of conduct and responsibility and appear to have the strings which control time, labor, and the generations in their hands. The Nation must now repair 10 years of errors, disorder, and confusion . . .

If anyone had undertaken the task of purposely wrecking our

economy and annihilating its dynamic forces, he could not have accomplished it in a more complete manner.

Today the people face the task of rebuilding the Nation. They have tremendous energies with which to overcome the serious difficulties. But it is vital that they understand in a coldly frank manner the extent and causes of the damage. We will know how to find solutions, and we will start immediately. We will vigorously attack the problem of our foreign indebtedness, and positive measures to combat inflation will be taken . . .

However, the Nation should not expect miracles or easy solutions. The inroads which have been made are very serious, but we will know how to offset them with firmness and decision, if the people support us . . .

8. *Aramburu Supplants Lonardi*

[Speech to the Nation by Gen. Pedro Eugenio Aramburu, broadcast immediately after he took his oath of office as President of the Provisional Government of Argentina, LRA Buenos Aires (Official), Argentine Home Service, Nov. 13, 1955, 8:40 p.m.]

People of Argentina: At this time, in view of difficulties which he was not able to overcome, Gen. Lonardi has returned to the Armed Forces the responsibility of selecting a new interpreter of the revolutionary idea. The manner in which he did this once more recommends him to his fellow citizens. The aims which had prompted military men and civilians to rise against a regime contrary to our traditions and our democratic way of life have already been presented by Gen. Lonardi to the people of Argentina in his message-program when he took over the Provisional Presidency on Sept. 23. These aims were then ratified in several official documents and in a speech which was delivered a very short time ago by Rear Admiral Rojas at the installation of the Consultative Council. (Applause)

A single idea animates the revolutionary movement. It is the democratic feeling of our people which burst into flower in 1810, and was reborn after the Battle of Caseros.[1] (Applause) Nothing could alter this line of behavior in the men who had assumed the historic responsibility of the hour. We want to confirm our purpose once more: The task of reestablishing the reign of law and the return of the country to its genuine democracy must be entrusted to men who, throughout their lives and on their past record, constitute the most solid guarantee of fulfillment of their aims. (Applause) Should we do otherwise, even if inspired by the best intentions, we would commit an error which would not be forgiven by a public opinion shaken by the anguish of past sufferings, wounded feelings, and spilled blood. (Applause) We know the support the Argentine people give these principles, and we want to give them absolute assurance that they will be maintained. (Applause) We also believe that these men with clean records are the best to carry to the public the assurance that the workers will have their rights guaranteed and that their conquests will be maintained and even enlarged. (Applause)

The sacrifice which our financial condition imposes upon the country must be borne by all, but in an equitable manner, determined by the abilities of each person. (Applause) In an atmosphere of reconquered freedom, the Argentine people must find many reasons for the expression of their religious feelings. And finally, we call upon all the inhabitants of the Republic to put aside all party and tendentious interests, in the higher interest of all. (Applause) May they all be guided by republican austerity, and may solidarity in common effort allow us quickly to reach the goals which we have set for ourselves . . .

9. *Why Lonardi Was Ousted*

[Communiqué from the office of Provisional President Aramburu, LRA Buenos Aires, in Spanish to Argentina, Nov. 14, 1955, 2:50 a.m.]

---

[1] The battle on February 3, 1852, which overthrew the tyrant Juan Manuel de Rosas.

It is normal for a democratic government to give publicity to its acts and in order to do so there is nothing better than the actual admission of facts.

The aims of the liberating revolution were set forth in the message of Gen. Lonardi when he assumed, in the name of the Armed Forces of the Nation, the Provisional Presidency of the Government. These aims were ratified today in the message which Provisional President Pedro Eugenio Aramburu addressed to the people of the Republic.

The Government crisis was not due to any change in these aims. The difference which caused Gen. Lonardi to return his prerogatives to the Armed Forces was due to a difference of opinion over the choice of persons who are to execute the Governmental acts. This, and this alone, was the reason for the much-discussed discrepancy. On Saturday, Nov. 12, Gen. Lonardi communicated to the Minister of the Interior and Justice his intention of dividing the Ministry and handing the Portfolio of the Interior to Dr. Luis María de Pablo Pardo. He proposed that Dr. Busso remain as Minister of Justice, an offer which the latter declined. A few hours later Gen. Lonardi offered the Ministry of Justice to Dr. Bernardo Velarde Irigoyen.

These acts provoked immediate disapproval from the Armed Forces, Government officials, and public opinion, and caused the resignation of the National Consultative Council composed of representatives of the Unión Cívica Radical, the National Democratic, Socialist, Progressive Democratic, and Christian Democratic Parties—the only exception being the representatives of the Christian Democratic Federal Union.

[The resigning representatives announced that] they considered that this Ministry should be and was being held by a citizen whose high intellectual gifts, added to his unalterable democratic ideas, represented full guarantees to all citizens. Since Lonardi persisted in his point of view, when a crisis arose over the question he decided to return his prerogatives to the Armed Forces which, with absolute unity of opinion, entrusted the high office to Gen. Pedro Eugenio Aramburu . . .

10. *Aramburu's Policies*

[Speech by Provisional President Gen. Pedro Eugenio Aramburu broadcast direct from the Government Palace. LRA Buenos Aires (Official), Argentine Home Service, Nov. 23, 1955, 0:22 a.m.]

Urgent tasks of the most varied nature and close attention demanded by events easily understood after having done away with a dictatorship which had punished the country for over 10 years, have prevented me from speaking to you since the day I took my oath as Provisional President.

On that occasion my words were brief, but they were sufficient to define the spirit which moves me in the task ahead and to establish the feelings of the Government over which I preside with unanimous and enthusiastic support of the Armed Forces of the Nation.

These forces are fully and absolutely identified with the supreme ideal of the fatherland, the standards of their glorious past, and their hope and will are directed to the purpose of restoring their moral hierarchy on the basis of democracy, which has meant the greatness of all free peoples among which, once more, we proudly occupy our traditional place.

As Commander in Chief of all Armed Forces, I am pleased to point out, with firmness and conviction, this solidarity in the ranks in the face of the demands of the revolution. I also take pleasure in stressing their exemplary conduct in the circumstances in which they had to work in order to guarantee to the people their right to work. They have done so, and will do so again, without boasting but with unyielding fortitude, conscious of their responsibility in these times in which we try to return and to assure to the people the full enjoyment and exercise of their rights.

I am also pleased to point out, as something of the utmost importance, the faith of all members of the Armed Forces in the democratic presentation of the Government. This fact gives me satisfaction and I rejoice, together with all my comrades of the Army, Navy, and Air Force, over the meaningful and open support which is apparent in the ideas and actions, in the observations and initiative of the members of the National Consultative Council which, by the high character of its members, who have a long and honorable record in civic action, represent a highly valuable contribution to the common task of all Argentina.

The members of that council, representatives of the most varied shades of republican thought, have shown a clear understanding of the situation through which the country is now passing. By placing the higher interests of the nation over their own party interests, they lend to the Provisional Government their invaluable aid in the study of the most complex problems. Thus, within a framework of austere dignity and loyal harmony which had only been reached in the greatest crossroads of our history, the members of that council are now dealing with the Government's economic plans with the help of the Ministers of Finance, Industry, Commerce, Labor and Social Welfare, and Treasury, and of the economic adviser to the Executive Power. In addition, the National Consultative Council is now entrusted with the study of the legal status of the Government, and other problems of transcendent importance regarding which the Government hopes, with complete confidence, to receive their authoritative opinion.

Some measures which have already been adopted have served, as is shown by the healthy reaction obtained at home and abroad, to prove with facts that our declarations reflect deep convictions and our unyielding determination to carry them out in practice.

For example, regarding relations between capital and labor, a factor of primary importance in the life of our Nation, this Government had started action, with energy and calmness, toward leading them onto the road of legality, mutual trust, and respect.

The firm decision to assure the workers the social conquests obtained, and to increase their material and spiritual well-being as much as possible, has motivated, among other reasons, the intervention of the General Confederation of Labor. This measure was based on the certainty that the working classes need a large union organization which, above party passions of the moment, would be able to defend their legitimate interests impartially.

The Ministry of Labor and Social Welfare has started strong action aimed at preventing and punishing arbitrary or violent acts which cause harm to the whole country. This Ministry will see to it that no deviation will be able to compromise the calm of the working people and the cooperation and harmony which must prevail among the various sectors which work for national greatness and prosperity.

The Provisional Government demands from capital and from labor the greatest confidence and deliberation, assuring both of them that the Ministry of Labor and Social Welfare will act in the most impartial and fair understanding of the problems the solution of which may require the mediation of the State as the representative of all the people.

The decision to liquidate that totalitarian organ of mind corruption, of tortures for expression of thought, which was called Secretariat of Press and Information, is another step in the needed direction we have taken, and from which we shall not retreat one step. To do so would be to frustrate the hopes of the people, to go against their feelings, and to deny our own history, as the Interior Minister has said, interpreting the Government's feelings, when he publicly announced this liquidation.

Without sparing effort, and always following the clear and definite standards already defined, the Government will take other measures without delay, measures of equal importance and identical orientation, the purpose of which will be to continue giving shape to and making real the program which we have undertaken to carry out.

The government has now undertaken the task of producing new electoral statutes. The purpose of the Armed Forces is to establish institutional order and to insure the effective guarantees proper to our republican tradition. In order to achieve this purpose, it is imperative to have not only an adequate civic climate on the basis of the most complete freedom, but in addition the citizens must have the possibility of expressing their true will.

In the days following my assuming the Presidency, I have wanted, in order to fulfill this fundamental duty, to carry out the purpose indicated above. The reforms, already analyzed in general terms, will be submitted to the Consultative Council of political parties. I am certain that a new set of regulations which are based on truth, drafted with the participation of political parties, and guaranteed by the Armed Forces of the Nation, will greatly help the Government which the sovereign people elect to perform its constitutional function.

I do not want to speak any longer, although many things still remain to be said. The country has to see the facts. What we have done already undoubtedly indicates what is our thought and what is our inspiration. Events which will occur soon, perhaps even tomorrow, pursuant to the will of the Government over which I have the honor of presiding, will aid in consolidating the public support which we believe we have already won. As in the greatest hours of our history, I repeat the magnificent words of the preamble of the Constitution signed in Santa Fe in 1853, and I invoke the protection of God, source of all reason and justice, so that it will help us insure the benefits of freedom for ourselves, for our children, and for all the people of the world who may wish to live in Argentina. (Applause)

INDEX

Index